THE DIVINE MADNESS
OF PHILIP K. DICK

Photo by Tessa B. Dick. Used with permission.

THE DIVINE MADNESS
OF PHILIP K. DICK

Kyle Arnold

OXFORD
UNIVERSITY PRESS

OXFORD
UNIVERSITY PRESS

Oxford University Press is a department of the University of Oxford. It furthers
the University's objective of excellence in research, scholarship, and education
by publishing worldwide.Oxford is a registered trade mark of Oxford University
Press in the UK and certain other countries.

Published in the United States of America by Oxford University Press
198 Madison Avenue, New York, NY 10016, United States of America.

© Oxford University Press 2016

First Edition published in 2016

Library of Congress Cataloging-in-Publication Data
Arnold, Kyle.
The divine madness of Philip K. Dick / Kyle Arnold.
pages cm. — (Inner Lives series)
Includes bibliographical references and index.
ISBN 978-0-19-974325-4 (acid-free paper)
1. Dick, Philip K.—Psychology.   2. Dick, Philip K.—Family.   3. Science fiction,
American—History and criticism.   4. Psychology and literature.   I. Title.
PS3554.I3Z545 2016
813'.54—dc23
2015033239

9 8 7 6 5 4 3 2 1
Printed by Sheridan, USA

Inner Lives

SERIES EDITOR
William Todd Schultz

———

Dan P. McAdams
GEORGE W. BUSH AND THE REDEMPTIVE
DREAM: A PSYCHOLOGICAL PORTRAIT

William Todd Schultz
TINY TERROR: WHY TRUMAN CAPOTE (ALMOST)
WROTE ANSWERED PRAYERS

Tim Kasser
LUCY IN THE MIND OF LENNON

Kyle Arnold
THE DIVINE MADNESS OF PHILIP K. DICK

CONTENTS

ACKNOWLEDGMENTS

Many thanks to William Todd Schultz for his unflagging and thoughtful encouragement throughout the writing of this book. Thanks to George Atwood, who taught me psychobiography and whose wise guidance helped me overcome several impasses. Thanks to Kathleen Savino for her writerly advice and support. Thanks to Amanda Lowe for further opening my perspective to transpersonal conceptions of madness that proved invaluable in fully grasping the subject matter of this book, and to the East Coast Waking Down in Mutuality group for providing ongoing learning in this area. I want to also thank Steve Cullen, Tessa Dick and Gregg Rickman for helpful advice along the way.

THE DIVINE MADNESS
OF PHILIP K. DICK

| | 2-3-74

Just after Christmas in 1981, a scruffy science fiction writer named Philip K. Dick was excited to receive an invitation to visit the studio of the film *Blade Runner*, which was to be released a few months later. *Blade Runner* was the first of many major motion pictures based on Dick stories, and the only one filmed during his lifetime. While Dick was an industrious author and had published thirty-three novels, he was a poor man most of his life, and never had mingled with Hollywood glamour before. He'd been asked to visit the film set earlier, but it was far away and Dick, who had a history of near-fatal car accidents he attributed to his own wish to die, had largely given up on driving. An actor friend, Mary Wilson, told him to insist that the studio send a limo to fetch him, and they did so. Dick asked Wilson to accompany him, as he believed she was conversant enough with the film industry to help the anxious author navigate its unfamiliar rituals and personages. Dick was particularly nervous about meeting the director, Ridley Scott, whom he had scathingly criticized as unoriginal in a review of Scott's previous film, *Alien*. A mystical contemplative, Dick balked when he heard from Scott that *Blade Runner* would omit the spiritual themes so central to his writing. But despite all this, the two got along unexpectedly well, and photos of the meeting show them goofing off with big smiles. When Scott took Dick

1

into a screening room and showed him the first twenty minutes of the uncompleted dystopian sci-fi film, Dick was spellbound. When the lights went on, he exclaimed that watching the footage was like having a mirror held up to his mind.

What neither Scott nor most audiences of *Blade Runner* knew was that Dick's mind really was every bit as far out as what was on the screen, if not more so. Dick had grappled with madness, and self-depreciatingly referred to himself as a "flipped-out freak." When he saw the *Blade Runner* footage –which included a scene of a murderous android undergoing a psychological evaluation– he might have been reminded of the time he called the police during a bout of paranoid terror and warned them he was a machine who should be locked up. Dick not only wrote stories about androids, but sometimes was afraid he literally was one. There are many other instances of Dick's life imitating sci-fi, the most notorious of which was his declaration that in early 1974 he was zapped by a bright pink light that uploaded mystical information into his brain. He believed the source of the light was a benevolent entity he nicknamed "Zebra." Zebra, so called because it camouflaged itself by assuming the form of everyday objects, revealed Dick's world was not what it seemed. According to Zebra, time had been frozen in the year 50 A.D. by the machinations of the Roman Empire. The rest of history was an illusion. His mind awakened by the pink light of Zebra, Dick witnessed scenes from ancient Rome superimposed over his neighborhood. He heard a voice in his head uttering cryptic messages and felt guided by an other-worldly entity. He saw streams of red and gold energy reshaping his environment. Many of his visions were chilling, but they were also exhilarating. The stories Dick spent his life conjuring were now real. His identity was transformed. In Dick's mind, he was no longer just a sci-fi genre writer, but a mystical seer and prophet. Because Dick's visions of 1974 were most powerful in February and March of that year, he referred to them, collectively, as *2-3-74*. They have perplexed Dick fans and scholars ever since.

After 1974, the visions faded, and Dick tried to come to grips with his experience. Although wildly imaginative, Dick was also a chronic doubter. Skeptical of the revelations he received, he considered what he called the "minimum hypothesis": that it was all nothing but delusion. Dick struggled for years with the question of his own sanity. To be sure, he had a point: 2-3-74 included striking paranoid features. As I hope to show, however, it is best to classify 2-3-74 not as a delusional episode but as a complex *psycho-spiritual emergency*, an intense psychological breakthrough resembling mental breakdown. The term *emergency*, here, signifies both a crisis and an *emergence* of a more profound level of wholeness. If handled well, these powerful events can contribute to personal growth. If miscarried, they can be traumatizing. Dick was not able to resolve his psychospiritual crisis. After Zebra left him, he lapsed into despair and made a brutal suicide attempt. But the experience was so engrossing that Dick was unable to let it go. He couldn't stop writing about 2-3-74, producing a total of four novels about it: *VALIS, The Divine Invasion, Radio Free Albemuth*, and the uncompleted *Transmigration of Timothy Archer*. He also churned out, over the span of eight years, an eight-thousand-page piece of philosophical-religious exposition he called his *Exegesis*.

Of the numerous interpretations of 2-3-74 that Dick generated during his frenzied exegetical activity, most are dazzling but many spurious. The *Exegesis* is a remarkable achievement of the imagination. Its pages are crammed with intricate philosophical reasoning, Gnostic mysticism, Jungian psychology, and occultism, all intertwined with autobiography. Each section of the *Exegesis* offers new theories, new explanations of 2-3-74. Dick proposes that the intelligence behind the pink light may have been God, the KGB, a satellite, aliens, a first-century Christian named Thomas with whom he was in telepathic communication, the CIA, a version of himself from a different dimension, or possibly his deceased twin sister contacting him from the spirit world. Each new theory of 2-3-74 telescopes out into further possible theories, ad infinitum. Dick never settled.

In the chapters to come, I explore philosophical ideas alongside psychiatric concerns, not to minimize the former but to place them in context. One of the theories Dick entertained about 2-3-74 was that his visions might be symptoms of paranoid schizophrenia. Indeed, Dick's imagination often drifted in a paranoid direction. He asked neighbors to conceal his identity, complaining that the FBI, CIA, or KGB was after him. In 1971 he was admitted to Marin State Psychiatric Hospital for claiming he was being pursued by government agents. Close examination of the context of Dick's paranoid episodes, however, reveals they are most parsimoniously explained as byproducts of his voracious consumption of speed. Dick began taking prescription amphetamines for asthma as a child and later ingested massive doses to fuel the frenetic pace of his writing. Because of its impact on the dopamine system of the brain, amphetamine abuse often causes paranoia. Previous commentators have conjectured that Dick's paranoia was the result of drug use, but many have focused on the wrong drug: LSD. Although Dick took LSD occasionally, there is no evidence that he was a heavy user. Rather, it was his excessive use of *amphetamines* that most likely led to paranoia.

During the zenith of Dick's amphetamine-fueled paranoia in 1971, his house was mysteriously burglarized. He came home one evening to find his windows smashed, his reinforced file cabinet broken open, and pieces of asbestos littering the floor. The burglary, made legendary by a famous *Rolling Stone* article, was a baffling event that sparked Dick's passion for creative theorizing. Dick's imagination ran wild. Were the burglars CIA operatives, Black Panthers, or political thugs? To date, the burglary remains a mystery. Like 2-3-74, the 1971 break-in is a much-discussed unsolved riddle of Dick's life. In Chapter 6, I investigate the burglary and examine the theories Dick invented to explain it. It turns out there is only one plausible explanation for what happened: Dick did it himself.

Another topic I explore is the death of Dick's twin sister Jane, which happened when Dick was an infant. I probe this event not because I believe that a person's psychology is necessarily the product of his or her infancy. Rather, I do so because Dick literally tells readers, repeatedly, it is the key to understanding him. I follow where he points. Elements of the story of Jane's death, which I call Dick's *origin story*, recur throughout his writing. The essence of that story is that Jane died as a result of parental neglect, while Dick was miraculously rescued from the brink of death. As I show, the motifs of the dead twin, the inhumane parental figure, and miraculous yet equivocal rescue show up often in Dick's life and work. As Dick said to his biographer Gregg Rickman, he "re-enacted" Jane's story.

That said, in addition to Jane's death, I also address traumatic events later in Dick's life, including separations from his parents that left him with a lifelong terror of abandonment. Like many traumatized people, he was largely unable to establish secure attachments to others. Dick had stormy relationships that drove him to the brink of suicide. Yet, his history of trauma also contributed to his development as a spiritual contemplative. It is not unusual for traumatic experiences to awaken spiritual insights. To paraphrase Leonard Cohen, cracks are how the light gets in. Similarly, Dick's emotional wounds opened him to religious themes of universal suffering and compassion. In Chapter 4, I take a developmental perspective on Dick's spirituality, closely examining scenes from his early life he identifies as spiritually formative. I make the case that his early traumas helped him develop a facility for profound empathy and for entering dissociative trancelike states of mind, both of which contributed to his psychospiritual crisis of 2-3-74.

My approach to Dick is broadly phenomenological, meaning that I delve deeply into his subjective frame of reference. I linger over the details of his inner life, in all its twists and turns. I spend more time *describing* Dick's psychology, bringing out its meaning from within, than *explaining* it. Take note: readers unwilling to enter the complex labyrinth of the mind of Philip K. Dick might best stop here. I also make use of context, trying to get a read on 2-3-74 by placing it in the big picture of Dick's life. I meticulously inspect the span of his life leading up to 2-3-74, as well as what happened afterward, in order to get clear on the difference between the overall weirdness inherent in being Philip K. Dick and the more specific weirdness of 2-3-74. And so, the following chapters include a close reading of the last eighteen years of Dick's life: a portrait of Dick in his late thirties and forties.

In some respects, Dick is his own best psychobiographer. A veteran therapy patient and avid reader of psychoanalytic literature, he was a keen observer of his own emotional life. I stay close to Dick's self-understanding, anchoring my observations in his self-analyses whenever possible. However, because he had blind spots, his self-analysis was incomplete. In Chapters 5 and 6, I will take a hard look at Dick's darker side, not to malign him but to get a comprehensive picture of who he was in the years prior to 2-3-74. In accord with my principle of starting with Dick's understanding of himself, however, I begin with the event he says is most central to his life's story: the death of his twin, Jane.

2 | DIE MESSAGES

Philip Kindred Dick was born a fraternal twin, in Chicago, Illinois, on December 16, 1928, along with his sister Jane. Dick's mother, Dorothy, was an aspiring writer and feminist activist. She had Bright's disease, a chronic kidney disorder that, when active, left her bedridden for days at a time. She was frequently weak and sick. When well, she worked for the Department of Labor editing pamphlets. Dick's father, Edgar, an ex-Marine and World War I veteran, was an inspector for the Department of Agriculture. He visited farms to count livestock and ensure that their numbers did not exceed the permitted quota. Edgar brought a knife with him to these inspections. If he found an extra sheep, he killed it.

The couple met in Colorado, and married soon after Edgar returned from combat in World War I. A few years later, Edgar's job took the couple to Chicago, which in the 1920s was a notoriously dangerous city rife with organized crime. In the frigid winter of 1928, Philip and his twin sister Jane were born six weeks prematurely in Dorothy and Edgar's Chicago apartment. No one expected twins. Although Dorothy contacted a local doctor to help, she did not arrive on time. Edgar had to deliver the babies himself. "I knew how because I had delivered a lot of calves," he later said to Philip's wife Anne. Philip was born first, and Jane, his dark-haired twin, came second. The twins were tiny. Philip was four and one-quarter pounds, Jane three and one-half pounds. Dorothy would later tell Philip that both infants were so small that she was able to nestle them in a shoebox, an improvised incubator that she placed on the oven to keep the babies warm. According to Dorothy, Philip and his sister spent the first weeks of their lives sickly and malnourished because Dorothy was unable to produce enough milk for both children. In a letter to Philip that she describes as an apologetic "mea culpa," Dorothy writes: "For the first six weeks of your life, you were both starving to death because the (incompetent) doctor I had could not find the right formula for your food and because I was so ignorant I did not know how desperate your condition was. I did know things weren't right, but I didn't know how to get other help." Dorothy says the doctor could not explain how to feed the babies formula to replace the breast milk she could not provide. She sent for her mother to help, but when she arrived two weeks later she was overwhelmed. Edgar withdrew from the agonizing situation, taking refuge in a men's club. Meanwhile, Philip and his sister were slowly dying of starvation. To make matters worse, Dorothy accidentally burned Jane's leg with a hot water bottle when the twins were six weeks old. Much later, a few years before Philip's death, he was to have visions of a world savior, Tagore, whose burned legs were stigmata of the sins of mankind.

After Jane's burn, a miraculous series of events unfolded. By chance, a salesman for Met Life insurance stopped by, offering $50 life insurance policies for children along with a free home visit by a nurse. The Dicks took the salesman up on the offer. A generous reading would be that they took out the policies to secure medical care for their children. A less generous reading would be that they planned to take advantage of Philip and Jane's imminent deaths so they could collect the benefits. In any case, the nurse arrived a few days later and noticed that not only had Jane been badly burned, but both twins were so malnourished they were on the verge of death. Philip and his sister were rushed to the hospital. Jane died on the way there. Philip was assessed to be about a day from death, but in a stroke of luck, it happened that Chicago had the first premature infant care center in the United States, with an advanced incubator that was operated by a pediatrician named Julian Hess, who had invented the device. After Philip was placed in the incubator and fed formula, he stabilized and began to gain weight. A closer brush with death and a more miraculous rescue are hard to imagine. Not only did Philip come very near dying, but his twin, his fraternal double, didn't make it. If not for the family's chance encounter with the uncannily named Met Life salesman, if not for their proximity to the only medical facility in the United States with the ability to support premature infants, Dick would have died.

This story of Jane's death is Dick's psychological origin story. Dick retold it again and again, in interviews, personal conversations, letters, and journal entries. As I will show, its key narrative arc—*inhumane authority figures who want you dead*, a *deadly doubling*, and a *miraculous yet equivocal rescue*—recurs throughout Dick's life and stories. The inhumane authorities variously appear as neglectful parents, manipulative teachers, or scheming government officials. The deadly doubling motif shows up in characters such as doomed twins, android simulacra, and alien imposters. The miraculous yet equivocal rescue may be attempted, often incompletely, by Christlike savior figures, benign bosses, or kindly strangers. In what follows, readers may notice that when writing of these motifs, I do not always sharply distinguish between Dick's life story and his fiction. Core psychological threads tend to run through all levels of a life, macro and micro, fact and fiction. Dick lived the same themes he wrote about.

Dick's origin story both inspired and entrapped him. Dick's mother told it to him again and again while he grew up, so that it defined both his own identity and his place in the world. Because of his mother's repeated retellings of the story, Jane was an intensely present absence in Dick's childhood, bridging the real and the imagined. Thoughts of Jane were thoughts of someone who had never been fully real for Dick. Like science fiction, they were thoughts of what might have been, what should have been, and what was not. They were intimations of possibilities, of stifled alternative universes. Jane was a window to other worlds. Yet, for the most part, Dick could only gaze through the window, unable to pass through it. His creativity was catalyzed by longing. He compulsively reenacted his origin story throughout his life, repeatedly running afoul of authorities, chasing his deadly muse-twin in destructive relationships with women, and seeking salvation through a kind of desperate spirituality. As he writes in his journals, "the ultimate problem confronting me all my life has been the senseless injury to and neglect of my sister."

In some instances, only one or two elements of Dick's psychological origin story are evident, and in others, its full arc emerges. While analyzing layers of a story, literary critics sometimes use the analogy of the *palimpsest*: a scroll whose text is erased so that it can be used again, with the original writing still partially visible underneath. Dick's life and work are palimpsests, containing many complex events that, when examined closely, reveal underlying elements of the core themes of inhumane authorities, deadly doubling, and miraculous but equivocal rescue.

To be sure, Dick's life cannot be reduced to the above themes. As we will see, Dick's life and his madness were complex and manifold. However, Dick himself points, emphatically, to the importance of his origin story for understanding his life history. He told his biographer Gregg Rickman that "in any real in-depth biography of me or any real in-depth study of me as a person, this is really the origin . . . if there can be said to be a tragic theme running through my life, it's the death of my twin sister and the re-enactment of this over and over again . . . *My psychological problems are traceable to the loss of my sister.*" To be sure, Dick did not retain any conscious memory of his sister's death, and psychological science has yet to fully clarify the mechanisms by which experiences in early infancy might contribute to the shaping of an adult personality. We know, however, that even very early experiences can have a dramatic impact on later development. Malnutrition is well documented to interfere with the growth of the nervous system, and disruptions in attachments in infancy are associated with later problems in the regulation of emotion in adult relationships. In a 1971 journal entry, Dick writes, "I can only be safe when sheltered by a woman . . . It is that I fear that I will simply die. My breath, my heart will stop. I will expire like an exposed baby. Jane, it happened to you and I am still afraid it will happen to me. They can't protect us . . ." Dick believed his sister's death had a direct relationship to his attachment anxieties, and there is a good chance he was right.

Inhumane Authorities

Even if one were to take a position of hardline skepticism and dismiss Dick's belief that Jane's death had a direct impact on him, the fact remains that it had a devastating impact on his parents, Dorothy and Edgar. Through their memories of Jane, she haunted Dick's childhood. Throughout Dick's life, Jane was a fraught topic of conversation with his mother. Dorothy led him to believe she held him responsible for Jane's death. She claimed she gave more of her breast milk to Dick because he was always hungry, leading to Jane's starvation. Dick would later say to his wife Tessa, "I heard about Jane a lot, and it wasn't good for me. I felt guilty— somehow I got all the milk." Dick felt Dorothy "hated" him. In an interview, he elaborates: "all those years she'd [Dorothy] make sure I knew about that dead child. My twin . . . And said 'It's a good thing she's dead.' And the rest of that message is, 'And why aren't you dead?' Meaning me. That's how I read that message." When Dick was an adult stricken by paranoia, he fearfully imagined that he was receiving "die messages," subliminal commands that he should die, from unknown forces. Dick's remarks about his mother indicate the original sender of the die messages was Dorothy. Directly and indirectly, she communicated to Dick not only that she wished he had died, but that in a fundamental moral sense he *should* have died. In other words, his existence itself was a moral transgression. By the mere fact of living, the die messages said, Dick killed his sister. *His life was inherently homicidal.* He was better off dead.

There is no way to prove Dick's mother wanted him dead, but the evidence is striking. Her neglect and the life insurance policy suggest that at the very least, she felt unable to cope with the responsibility of caring for him. It is, in fact, not uncommon for overwhelmed mothers to harbor death wishes against their children. The nursery rhyme "Rock-a-bye Baby" famously illustrates these wishes in its last line: "When the bough breaks the cradle will fall, and down will come baby, cradle and all." Parents may be relatively unaware of these infanticidal wishes, or occasionally conscious of them. Infanticidal wishes are rarely acted upon. In some circumstances, however, they can contribute to neglect, which is likely what happened to Dick. Whatever his mother's true feelings, there is no doubt Dick *perceived* her as someone who wanted him dead. In interviews, letters, and conversations, he says so again and again, consistently and unambiguously.

Dorothy's die messages also show up in Dick's stories, in cryptic yet unmistakable form. Take his horror/sci-fi story "The Hanging Stranger." In "The Hanging Stranger," an everyman, Ed Loyce, notices a "shapeless dark bundle" hanging from a lamppost. Fascinated and concerned, Loyce takes a closer look. The "hackles on his neck" rise as Loyce slowly realizes the bundle is the corpse of a stranger, bloody and disfigured. He tries to notify others, but they seem oblivious. Investigating further, Loyce discovers that the entire town has been hypnotized by aliens who mimic the human form. He flees to another town, and warns an official identified only as the "Commissioner." Loyce is informed the hanging body is "bait" to expose free individuals who were not hypnotized, like himself. It becomes immediately clear that the Commissioner is actually an alien in disguise, and that Loyce has been captured.

Loyce is led outside toward a rope, which is to be the site of his own hanging. Loyce's corpse is to be the next piece of bait, used to snare the next free human. Thus the cycle continues.

Note the sequence of Loyce's death. By noticing the hanging body, Loyce sets his own death in motion. His death is triggered on page one of the story, as soon as he identifies the dark bundle as a body. The bait has already got him. Moreover, the specific mode of Loyce's death is to become a hanging stranger himself. When he sees the hanging stranger, he is, in essence, encountering his own death. The hanging body is an echo from Loyce's future. *The die message is a program that initiates when you notice, in some form, your own death.* Your present and your future suddenly lock together. As soon as you see your death, you are programmed to die. Think of the core message Dick received from his mother: *you should be dead.* The message implies both that you are *supposed to* be dead, and maybe you *are* dead. In most of Dick's stories, it is a deadly double, a dead or homicidal alter ego, that activates the die message.

Dick's father, Edgar, did not convey die messages like Dorothy did. Most accounts of Dick's childhood portray Edgar as gentle yet detached. To quote Edgar, he "had a difficult time learning to know and understand the strange actions of creatures called people." As an adult Dick tended to depict his relationship with Edgar as largely free of strife, at least in comparison with Dorothy. "I got along very well with my father, but I really hated my mother," Dick told Rickman. That said, Edgar was not of much help in providing a buffer between the young Philip Dick and his traumatized mother. As mentioned before, Edgar worked for the U.S. Department of Agriculture as an inspector for a program that maintained livestock prices by restricting the sizes of herds. His job required him to spend much of his time on the road, visiting farms all across California. In short, Edgar was often absent. Moreover, even when he was around, Edgar flooded Dick with anxieties. According to Tessa, Dick said his father often woke him up in the dead of night, put him in the car, and drove east at breakneck speed, exclaiming that a devastating earthquake was about to occur. Had Edgar dreamed of an earthquake, and been unable to distinguish reality from dream? Or was he sometimes utterly delusional? We don't know the answer to these questions. It was equally distressing to the young Dick when Edgar terrified his son with stories of his wartime exploits. He had kept a WWI gas mask, and liked to put it on and frighten Dick. Dick later said, "As a child I felt a lot of anxiety listening to my father's war stories . . . what scared me the most was when my father would put on the gas mask. His face would disappear. This was not my father any longer. This was not a human being at all." In 1963, many years after the gas mask conversations with his father, the adult Philip Dick was reminded of them when, walking alone in the country, he had a terrifying vision of a "vast visage of evil" filling the sky. Like Edgar's mask, it had "empty slots for eyes" and was "metal and cruel." "Worst of all," Dick reported, "it was god."

Dick wrote a story entitled "The Father-Thing," about a boy whose father is replaced by a malevolent extraterrestrial entity. In the story, a boy named Charles goes to fetch his father for dinner and finds him speaking to an identical duplicate. Puzzled, he returns to the dinner table, and is terrified when the duplicate walks in and starts eating. Investigating, he discovers the empty skin of his real father, the insides having been eaten by the duplicate. The father-thing tries to hunt Charles down, but he escapes. Charles discovers that the father-thing is being remotely controlled by a small spiderlike alien, and is able to kill it. Released from control, the father-thing collapses in a heap. In "The Father-Thing," the themes of deadly doubling and inhumane authorities coincide. The Father-Thing is an inhumane authority because it is a deadly double.

When Dick was five years old, his parents divorced. Dick was not to see his father for another six years. It was another loss, this time one that was most certainly directly felt. Dick had lost a sister and now a father. Even worse, the loss of income meant his mother had to work full time, and to free up her time to do so, she sent Dick away to boarding school. Now, Dick had lost everyone. He developed anorexia and malnutrition. Dick's eating disorder became severe enough to warrant clinical attention. "I was literally starving," he later said. To eat meant to get all the milk, which, according to Dorothy, meant to kill Jane. Dick had internalized Dorothy's die messages. Eating was killing, killing was eating. The authorities at the boarding school did not understand him and were unable to help, sending Dick home. After Dick returned home, his mother took him to a psychiatrist, and Dick participated in psychotherapy on and off for most of his life. It was a kind of rescue, but as it nearly always would be for Dick, an equivocal one. Psychotherapy helped Dick attain insight into himself, but it never seemed to touch the underlying problem. Dick's resistance to health is understandable, as any move toward life contradicted his internalized die messages. He wasn't supposed to get better. He wasn't even supposed to have lived.

Indeed, when Dick's parents buried his sister, they engraved Dick's name on the tombstone next to Jane's name. Under both names is engraved the word "Twins." It is as if, consciously or not, Dick's parents had authored his identity by writing it on his twin sister's grave. We don't know what their conscious rationale was for this decision. Perhaps, Dick being as sickly as he was, they expected him to die young, and impoverished as the family was, they may not have been able to afford an additional grave. Yet whatever Dick's parents' reasoning was, the gravesite's implicit message to Philip was that he was supposed to be dead, like his sister. They were meant to be together in death. It was written in stone.

As for Dick's eating disorder, he was to have it for the rest of his life, and was often unable to eat when there was another person in the same room. Dick later developed several other related anxieties. Starting in his teenage years, he had bouts of vertigo triggered by fear of death. Describing it, Dick wrote in a letter, "The real fear, then, is that you yourself—which at one time did not exist— *may again not exist;* fear inside you, flooding over you in wave after wave of panic, is what is experienced as an engulfing of that self."

Deadly Doubling

Overwhelming fear of death is a common experience for those who have lost a close family member. This is partly because the death of a family member confronts a person with the inevitability of his or her own death. However, there is also another reason. Individuals who lose a family member early in life typically develop fantasies of identification with the deceased, and a terror of joining the deceased in death. With the death of a twin, it is to be expected that these fantasies of identity should be especially powerful.

In Dick's 1954 short story "Upon the Dull Earth," a girl named Silvia learns to summon angels by means of sheep's blood. She accidentally cuts herself, and the angels are drawn to her blood. These inhumane authorities destroy her body and pull her into the afterlife. Silvia's lover, Rick, cannot accept her death, and demands that the angels restore her to life: an attempt at miraculous rescue. But as always, the miraculous rescue is only a partial success. When the angels try to restore Silvia to life, something goes wrong and she is reincarnated in the body of her sister Betty Lou. Soon, the bodies of the rest of Silvia's family transform into identical duplicates of Silvia, all uttering variations of Silvia's last words before dying, "Oh! I cut myself. On a nail or something." Rick flees, but everyone he sees is quickly changed into a copy of Silvia. Exhausted, Rick returns to his apartment, and upon looking in the bathroom mirror, finds that the face looking back at him is Silvia's. When the story ends, the newly copied Sylvia collapses into a chair, crying plaintively for Rick's help. The narrative describes identification gone wrong. Identification resurrects Silvia, but imperfectly, and at the price of destroying the identities of her loved ones.

One of the most sophisticated accounts of identifications that occur in reaction to losses can be found in a famous paper by the French psychoanalysts Nicholas Abraham and Marie Torok entitled "The lost object—me: Notes on endocryptic identification." To deal with an overwhelming loss, the child may establish an "intrapsychic crypt" in his or her mind, a closed-off domain of mental life that includes fantasies of the lost other. Secretly, the child develops elaborate fantasies of interacting with the deceased. In Dick's case, he developed a series of imaginary friends based on his fantasies of Jane. Tessa reports that Dick imagined that, had his sister Jane lived, she would have grown into a girl who was "small, with dark eyes and long dark hair. She was also very gutsy, always daring Phil to do things he was afraid of, helping him to get into trouble." In an interview, Dick said he often imagined the young Jane in a wheelchair, presumably because of her leg injury.

Abraham and Torok argue that the intrapsychic crypt both denies the reality of the loss and maintains an imaginary connection with the deceased. But the plot thickens, for in the crypt, a psychological switch-off occurs in which the individual afflicted by loss identifies with the deceased so strongly that he or she can start to feel like the one who has been lost—so that it is he or she, not the deceased, who is felt to be missed. In other words, the child (in this case Dick) feels as if he *is* the person he has lost (Jane) and thus feels he has lost not Jane but *himself*. This cryptic dynamic is challenging to grasp but useful in understanding the *deadly doubling* aspect of Dick's origin story. One Dick twin died, and the other survived. The point is, Dick could identify with *either* twin. Sometimes he felt like the dead twin, and other times like the survivor. Although this notion might seem hard to prove, Dick explicitly spells it out. He writes in 1978 of a "two part oscillation of my total existence: (1) The part where I am alive in this world & my sister is dead & an idea in my brain; & (2) the other part where I am dead & she is alive & I am a thought in her living brain . . ." A clearer statement of Abraham and Torok's theory would be hard to imagine.

Images of intrapsychic crypts show up in several of Dick's stories. In one of his most respected novels, the award-winning *Ubik*, a group of security agents is deployed to protect a lunar installation from attack by telepaths. A bomb explodes, apparently killing the chief of the security agency, Glen Runciter. After the explosion, the agents notice odd discrepancies and shifts in the fabric of reality. Runciter's face shows up on coins, and messages from him appear scrawled on bathroom walls. Time reverses and objects retrogress, cars and elevators transforming into older models of themselves. Eventually, the characters realize that, in fact, Runciter did not die in the bomb explosion but was the sole survivor. The rest of the group has nearly died, their bodies cryogenically frozen on the verge of death, so that their minds can only be reached from the outside world by Runciter's telepathic communications. Runciter transmits to them a substance called Ubik, which prevents objects from retrogressing in time and deteriorating. The effects of Ubik are only temporary, however, making Ubik another equivocal rescue to add to the list. At the end of the story, Runciter notices the face of one of the agents, Joe Chip, on a coin. This suggests the scenario has reversed again. Did Runciter die, after all? Is he the one who was cryogenically frozen, and Joe Chip the survivor? We can discern here a version of the "two part oscillation" Dick describes between life and death: a cryptic fantasy in which one cannot decide whether the deceased is oneself or someone else. In the novel, the dilemma is never fully resolved. We never find out who is really dead.

In another of Dick's novels, *Dr. Bloodmoney, Or How We Got Along After the Bomb*, Dick portrays a young girl, Edie Keller, with a twin, Bill. Bill is a fetus in fetu, a conjoined twin who developed inside Edie's body. Bill is in telepathic communication with the dead and with Edie. Like the cryogenically frozen security agents in Ubik, Bill resides in an insulated internal world that is in the neighborhood of the dead. The literary critic Katherine Hayles notes in her 1999 paper "Turning reality inside out and right side out" that Edie and Bill's relationship is a reversal of Philip and Jane's relationship, as if it were Jane who carried the dead Philip's spirit within her rather than vice versa. As Hayles puts it, "Edie and Bill are Dick and Jane turned inside out." I would add that Bill's hidden dwelling within Edie's body vividly illustrates the structure of an intrapsychic crypt as described by Abraham and Torok: a cut-off internal space linked to the dead.

Although it is unlikely Dick read Abraham and Torok's work, he was fascinated with death-related concepts that appear in the writings of another psychoanalyst, Ludwig Binswanger. Binswanger, a German psychiatrist, developed an alternative version of psychoanalysis inspired by the existential philosophy of Martin Heidegger. An existential psychiatrist, Binswanger believed psychiatric conditions are best understood not through scientific experimentation or diagnosis but through close analysis of the subjective experience of patients. Accordingly, Binswanger devoted himself to detailing the worlds of experience that patient inhabit and describing how specific problems crystallize out of these experiential worlds. Dick delved deeply into Binswanger's paper "The Case of Ellen West," in which Binswanger describes a suicidal patient riven between an "ethereal world" of light and joy and a "tomb world" of stale decay and death.

Dick alludes to Binswanger's tomb world in a number of his works, such as his most famous novel, *Do Androids Dream of Electric Sheep?* In *Androids*, Dick invents a religion called Mercerism, whose disciples worship by activating a device known as an "empathy box." The empathy box enables Mercerists to emotionally fuse with their messiah, Mercer, who in turn is a symbol of all living things. Mercer is a Sisyphus-like figure, an elderly man fated to ascend a mythical hill while unseen persecutors throw rocks at him, and to be struck down after his ascension is complete. When Mercer is knocked down, he lands in a tomb world filled with bones and "rotting fragments," in which time has slowed to a near halt. Almost imperceptibly, the bones and fragments return to life, and Mercer climbs out of the tomb world and starts back up the hill. In his *Exegesis*, Dick referred to "my twin sister Jane" as a "post mortem world" that "has been with me all my life." From this perspective, Mercer's journey alludes to Dick's emotional struggle to negotiate the "post mortem world" into which he was thrown by his imaginary identification with Jane. Mercer, then, is Dick himself, symbolically reenacting (as he put it) the death of his twin sister and resurrecting her in fantasy, over and over again.

Dick's tomb world was a site not only of death but also, potentially, of alienation. In *Martian Time-Slip*, Dick describes Manfred Steiner, a ten-year-old mentally ill boy with precognitive abilities. In the world as Steiner sees it, the destructive progression of time is accentuated. When Steiner looks at another character, Arnie Kott, he sees "dead bones, shiny and wet. Mr. Kott was a sack of bones, dirty and yet shiny-wet. His head was a skull that took in greens and bit them; inside him the greens became rotten things as something ate them to make them dead." Steiner's unyielding perception of death and dying renders it almost impossible for him to communicate with other human beings, because Steiner perceives them as horrific walking corpses who emit only "gubbish."

Dick's feelings about his deceased twin not only emerged in his stories, but also contributed to repetitive patterns in his relationships with the living women in his life. Dick was married five times, and many of his relationships were conflictual. He was terrified of losing his spouses, and even the slightest hint of tension in these relationships triggered overwhelming fears of separation. When relationships ended, Dick was devastated. At least twice, he made suicide attempts after relationships had broken up. According to Dick, he obsessively turned to his image of his twin sister when selecting romantic partners. He even claimed to have once dated a woman solely because she was named "Jane."

As an adult, Dick fetishized this image of his twin, referring to an archetypically seductive "dark-haired girl." In a paper entitled "The Evolution of a Vital Love," Dick outlines the development of his attraction to the dark-haired girl. He relates that throughout much of his life his romantic choices were alluring yet cold younger women, who falsely gave the impression of emotional warmth because of "intense black hair and black eyes." Dick had infatuations with a long series of women with these characteristics. He characterizes them as androids, creatures who are intelligent but lack empathy. They are both dead and deadly, fictionalized versions of the deadly doubling motif found in Dick's origin story. One of these dark-haired girls, Linda Levy, recounts that Dick would "reel from passing remarks and obsess over them." At times, she says, he would "curl up into a ball, eyes empty, cold and silent . . ." When Dick emerged from these states of cold withdrawal, his behavior was unpredictable and occasionally violent. Levy reports that once, while she and Dick were driving home from a movie, she mentioned to Dick that she had made plans with another science fiction writer, Norman Spinrad. Probably feeling abandoned, Dick withdrew into cold silence. He then, Levy says, grabbed hold of the steering wheel and swerved the car into oncoming traffic. Levy managed to wrench the wheel away from Dick and steer the car safely to the curb.

Some critics, such as Ursula Le Guin, accused Dick of misogyny. Indeed, his stories are filled with unsympathetic female characters that are seductive and self-centered. For instance, in *Do Androids Dream of Electric Sheep?*, the protagonist of the story, Rick Deckard, gets romantically involved with a female android, Rachel Rosen, whom he initially believes to be human. Deckard, a bounty hunter who makes a living by destroying androids, then discovers his feelings for Rachel could inhibit him from killing other androids. Rachel reveals that this was her purpose all along, and that she seduced several other bounty hunters to render them incapable of android hunting. Later in the story, Rick kills an android that is an identical copy of Rachel Rosen.

Dick made no secret of his conflicted feelings about women, and often traced them to his mother. Dick depicted her as coldly unfeeling and manipulative: an android. According to a male friend, Dick called his mother the "dark witch of the universe." Part of the problem was that Dorothy was ill much of the time with kidney disease. A family friend compared her medicine cabinet to a small pharmacy. During bouts of illness, Dorothy isolated herself in her bedroom, irritable and depressed. Dorothy's day-to-day life was one of pain and helplessness. Dorothy's stepdaughter, Lynne Hudner, reported that there was always "an undercurrent of suffering and limitation that created an atmosphere of heaviness and somberness in Dorothy's household." Hudner also says Dorothy, making the best of a bad diagnosis, used her illness to manipulate her family. If so, it must have been challenging for the young Philip Dick to determine how much of his mother's suffering was bona fide, and how much of it was exaggeration.

In addition to the ongoing stress of her medical problems, Dorothy never recovered from Jane's death. Dick's wife Anne, who was introduced to Dorothy when she was in her fifties, writes that at that time Dorothy still "spoke of Jane ... as though Jane had died only yesterday." Over twenty years after Jane died, the wound was still raw. Dorothy later disclosed, in letters to Dick, that she blamed herself for Jane's death. That seems to be the key to understanding how she treated him. Dorothy was plagued by guilt about Jane's death, and coped by deflecting her guilt onto Dick. She could not bear to think that she had killed her own infant, so pointed the finger at Dick. Whether Dorothy objectively was or was not to blame for Jane's death, she *felt* blameworthy. From an early age, then, Dick was entangled in Dorothy's defensive attempts to exonerate herself. He was used as a piece on her defensive chessboard. Her opponent: her own guilty conscience.

Miraculous yet Equivocal Rescue

The story of Dick's rescue from imminent starvation as an infant is stunning. He came within a day of death, and his survival was contingent on a cluster of slim chances. If not for the serendipitous encounter with the life insurance salesman, if not for the fact that Met Life happened to include nursing services, if not for the fact that the family lived in the city with the United States' first premature infant care center -staffed by the very individual who had invented the incubator- Dick would have died. Yet, not only was Dick's rescue a close shave, it also left him with a difficult fate. His twin sister was dead, making the rescue a partial success only. Moreover, Dick was rescued from death only to absorb the negative impact of his mother's die messages and his father's war trauma.

In Dick's stories, the rescue sometimes is equivocal because it is a trap. In "The Hanging Stranger," Loyce miraculously escapes an entire town bent on his destruction, only to find that his safe haven is the site of his execution. In "Upon the Dull Earth" angels resurrect the dead Sylvia, but her endless copies replace everyone. In other stories, the rescue is equivocal because it may be an illusion. In *Do Androids Dream of Electric Sheep?* Deckard is protected from harm by a savior figure, Mercer, who may be an illusion. In *Ubik*, the telepathic heroes of the story are temporarily rescued by the miraculous titular substance, Ubik, but by the story's end, it appears that reality itself may have collapsed.

Although these equivocal rescues are fictional constructions, they also allude to Dick's life pattern. Dick, we will see, spent much of his life pining for rescue from the reality of an existence that felt both painful and false. He felt trapped. The shape of the trap varied, to be sure. When Dick was young, he was imprisoned in a painful family environment, and later, in boarding school. As an adult, Dick felt trapped in a series of unhappy marriages, a grueling career, and massive debt. Each new relationship seemed to repeat his origin story, with romantic partners assuming the roles of vulnerable twin sister or neglectful mother. Part of the trap was that the *equivocal rescue* component of the story provided a built-in mirage of an exit door that appeared a *way out of* Dick's life pattern but was actually a *basic part of* the pattern. By its very nature, Dick's origin story included an illusory exit.

3 | RETREAT SYNDROME

The death of Dick's twin sister was just the beginning of a lifetime of trauma. His later childhood was also marred by neglect and conflict. Dick's father, Edgar, flip-flopped between attitudes of gentle detachment and frightening rage. Dick writes in a 1976 letter: "I was very much afraid of my father, and sometimes he seemed to me to be someone else entirely, not *my* father but another person pretending to be him." It seemed to him as if his good father would disappear, an evil one appearing in his place. Psychologists call this phenomenon *splitting*. Splitting often happens in conflictual families when children fear that the negative feelings in their relationships with parents will overwhelm the positive feelings. In splitting, the child protects positive feelings by sequestering off negative feelings as if the latter were in reference to another person entirely.

When Dick was four years old, his parents separated. Edgar was transferred to a job in Reno, Nevada, but Dorothy refused to accompany him there because she was concerned the Reno job might be short-lived. As a compromise, Edgar stayed in Reno during the week and visited Dick and his mother on weekends. Edgar and Dorothy became distant. As Edgar tells the story, Dorothy withdrew as she began to enjoy the freedom she was afforded when he was away. However, Dorothy's stepdaughter Lynn Cecil offers an alternative perspective. Cecil says Edgar was jealous and possessive, flying into a rage if any man so much as glanced at Dorothy. It was Edgar's jealousy, Cecil asserts, that led Dorothy to leave him. The couple separated in 1933 and completed their legal divorce in 1935. Edgar faded out of Dick's life and disappeared. Dick was not to see his father again for another four years. He blamed his mother for driving him away. Unbeknownst to him, the absent Edgar had a protracted custody battle with Dorothy, claiming that because of his substantial income he was the more capable caregiver. Edgar failed to win custody of the young Dick, and he was raised in poverty by Dorothy. Dorothy moved in with her mother, who Dick called "Meemaw," in Berkeley, California. Meemaw cared for Dick while his mother went to work as a secretary. According to Dorothy, Meemaw indulged Dick whereas Dorothy withheld affection. Meemaw's husband, Earl, came to live with the family in 1934 when Dick was five years old. Dick later depicted Earl as a gigantic, intimidating redneck.

In 1935, Dorothy moved to Washington, D.C., where she had secured a better-paying job writing bulletins on childcare for the Children's Bureau of the Department of Labor. Dorothy brought Dick to Washington, leaving Meemaw and Earl in California. Dick had been wrenched away from his father when four years old, left in the care of his grandmother while his mother worked, and now at five, he was abruptly separated from his grandmother too. Moreover, Dick's mother spent most of the day at work, relying on maids and friends to care for him. The series of ruptures in these early attachments took a psychological toll, and Dick developed severe anxiety with difficulty swallowing. He also had asthma. By age six, Dick was taking an amphetamine medication for asthma called ephedrine. Ephedrine was the first of many prescription drugs Dick was to use and abuse throughout his life, having been started on a trajectory of amphetamine use that would later result in paranoid delusions. Adding yet another traumatic separation to Dick's life, Dorothy decided to send him to boarding school. Dick later claimed the two had been staying with friends to save money, and Dorothy believed boarding school would provide a healthier environment for him. But in another account, Dick said he was a "problem child" and the school was intended for children with behavior problems. Dorothy enrolled Dick in Countryside School in Silver Spring, Maryland, for six months of his first-grade year.

Although it appears neither Dorothy nor Edgar was actively abusive toward the young Dick, the series of separations to which he was subjected suggests a passive and even neglectful attitude on the part of his parents. Although Dorothy retained custody of him, she placed him in the hands of various relatives, friends, and then a boarding school. As for Edgar, interviews with him give the impression he was oblivious to the impact of his absence on his son. Despite the fact that Edgar often was in Washington on business trips, he failed to visit Dick until he was eight years old, and gave no cogent explanation why. "What happened in Washington," Edgar said in an interview with biographer Gregg Rickman, "I don't know. She [Dorothy] moved away." After failing to get custody of Dick, Edgar checked out of his life. "We got divorced and I had my own life to live," Edgar explains, speaking as if his own life did not include his son.

Contemporary theories of trauma suggest trauma has two phases. In the first phase, a stressful event happens that overwhelms a person's ability to cope. The first phase of trauma, however, may not necessarily leave a psychological scar. If a traumatized child is surrounded by sensitive, supportive caregivers, the impact of the traumatic event can be cushioned. On the other hand, if the child's caregivers cannot respond sensitively to the traumatic experience, then their lack of empathy makes it harder for the child to process it. In the absence of parental support, the child's psyche is forced to cope with the memories of the traumatic event by dissociating these memories rather than digesting them. Dick's circumstances fit the latter scenario. Not only was he traumatized by repeated ruptures in his early attachments, but his feelings about them were ignored. Edgar put Dick out of his mind, and Dorothy handed him over to others. Dick was neglected and his feelings *about* being neglected were also neglected. It was neglect squared.

Dick did not fare well at boarding school. He was so distressed at the separation from his family that his anxiety worsened and he had more difficulty swallowing food. Difficulty swallowing often occurs in children with broken attachments, and Dick's were in tatters. He later said the only food he could force down his throat was a dog biscuit, which he would sneak from the school kitchen. He writes, "The boarding school could not handle me because I weighed less each month, and was never seen to eat a string bean." As Dick continued to waste away, the school authorities sent him home. Dick had learned a dangerous lesson: if in dire circumstances he neglected his own health dramatically enough, he would be rescued. Self-neglect became a weapon to conquer the neglect of others.

The rescue, though, was equivocal. Dick escaped the boarding school, but when he returned home his mother resumed her habit of entrusting his care to others, this time hiring a maid while she wrote childcare pamphlets. Dick complained that he waited alone for hours for Dorothy to return from work. During the rare moments Dorothy was available, Dick tried to get her attention with temper tantrums, but these were rarely effective in eliciting the needed care. Dick was eventually placed in a Quaker school, and in second grade transferred to public school. He continued to use the malingering technique he had stumbled on in boarding school, frequently faking illness in order to stay home. "The only way I survived school," Dick later wrote, "was to stay home sick and cheat a lot." School records state Dick was absent on twenty-four of the first thirty days of second grade. Most of Dick's grades are C's, although his teachers note that he showed talent in writing. Dick later boasted that he was so unpopular his classmates jeered and throw rocks at him, and that he took refuge under parked cars and growled back at them.

Dick's fantasy life bloomed under these pressures. He learned to use his mind to retreat from the pain of rejection by conjuring worlds of the imagination. In the absence of reliable family and friends, he invented imaginary companions. One imaginary friend, "Teddy," was inspired by his teddy bear, and perhaps also his father Edgar's nickname, "Ted." Dick pretended he was a cowboy riding a horse alongside his dead twin Jane, whom he imagined as a cowgirl. His short story "Retreat Syndrome" dramatizes the use of fantasy to withdraw from unbearable experiences. In "Retreat Syndrome," a man named John Cupertino discovers that the world around him is fake, a product of his imagination. When he is stopped by the police for speeding, he reaches for his registration only to find that his hand passes through the dashboard as if though thin air. The officers advise Cupertino to see his doctor, and when he does so, Cupertino discovers that he committed a terrible crime and withdrew into a delusional world to avoid facing it. In Dick's fantasy life, like Cupertino's, anything was possible. He could even resurrect his dead sister, undoing his belief that he was responsible for her death. Dick was training his mind to transmute reality into fiction.

In 1938, Dick and his mother moved back to Berkeley, California, to live near Meemaw again. Dorothy transferred to the Forestry Department, where she continued to work long hours and remained relatively unavailable to Dick. A friend, George Kohler, said she would come home late in the evening and Dick "just seemed to raise himself." Kohler reports that Dorothy was strict and as a result "he didn't really talk and tell her what he was thinking, or doing . . . he was afraid of criticism." Dick learned to hide his thoughts and feelings. At grammar school in Berkeley, Dick took on a new identity, assuming the nickname "Jim." Presumably, he wanted to put behind him the experiences of alienation and peer rejection he had suffered in Washington. Maybe if he left his name behind, too, he could make a fresh start. It worked. School reports from that period portray him as "original" and popular with classmates. Dick wrote several issues of a comical paper he called "The Daily Dick." Perhaps it was grammar school in Berkeley that planted the seeds of Dick's legendary charisma. He learned that if he wanted to fit in, he could simply turn the page and conjure up a new identity. Creativity could be used to generate popularity. Dick could win love by being a character.

His frequent absences from school continued, however. In addition to asthma, Dick now was diagnosed with tachycardia or rapid heartbeat. We can't be certain of what caused the tachycardia, but it is a good bet that the amphetamines Dick took for his asthma had something to do with it. To be sure, Dick later said his rapid heartbeat was a symptom of anxiety. Anxiety, though, is aggravated by amphetamine use. Drugs were starting to settle into a paradoxical role in Dick's life as both a cause and solution of his problems. Increasingly, they were both cure and curse.

Despite reports of Dick's boyhood popularity, friends perceived him as detached. One friend, Leon Rimov, said Dick was a "loner. Somewhere along the line he'd been. . . emotionally hurt . . . There was an absence of identity . . . He'd say 'I don't know why I'm here, I don't know where I belong, I don't know what I'm doing.'" I would underscore the phrase *absence of identity*. Disturbances of identity are common for neglected children. Identity, researchers have found, is an exquisitely relational phenomenon. We find out who we are by seeing ourselves reflected in the eyes of others. Children whose caregivers are neglectful or absent lack sufficient opportunities to see themselves in their caregivers' eyes, and as a result their identities are left unformed and insubstantial. As adults, they often complain of estrangement and emptiness—common complaints of the adult Philip K. Dick. A clinical term for Dick's emotional estrangement is *depersonalization*. Depersonalization is a radical form of detachment characterized by a pervasive feeling that the world is unreal and that one is observing it from a remote, third-person perspective, as if life were a movie. Dick's depersonalization was to do double duty in his adult life as both a source of existential pain and an inspiration for stories about simulated realities.

As a teenager Dick was awkward, although able to muster up bursts of charm. In a letter to his daughter, Dick describes what it was like for him to be a teenager: "the person senses that . . . this unique identity . . . may be snuffed out, may be engulfed by the world that confronts him or her, especially by all the other identities coming into existence on all sides. The real fear, then, is that you yourself—which at one time did not exist—may again not exist; fear inside you, flooding over you in wave after wave of panic, is what is experienced as an engulfing of that self." R. D. Laing, the existential psychiatrist, coined the term *ontological insecurity* for the kind of terrifying experience Dick describes. People who are ontologically insecure, Laing writes, feel unreal, deadened, and engulfed by others. Their fundamental sense of *being*—their ontology—is insecure. Although the evidence suggests that Dick was ontologically insecure since early childhood, he became acutely aware of that insecurity during his teenage years. Dick felt radically different from other people, as they seemed to possess a sense of solid existence that he lacked. In conversations with friends, he struggled to make sense out of human relationships, relying on his intellect to theorize about how to interact while his peers seemed to understand each other intuitively.

Dick continued to learn how to use his intellect to playfully deceive others and manipulate situations. He was a notorious prankster. While listening to a song with his friend Daniels, Dick convinced Daniels that it was composed by Tchaikovsky, whom Daniels hated. After Daniels denigrated the song, Dick revealed it was written by another composer. Dick enjoyed playing with his friends' sense of reality, much as he later would enjoy playing with his readers'. He was captivated by a comic book entitled *Mandrake the Magician*, about a magician superhero with the power to create illusions. In the comic, Mandrake uses the power of illusion to hypnotize and defeat criminals. Dick used the art of illusion to empower himself. Although Dick's own identity felt unreal, he could take solace in his ability to shape the realities of others.

The Philip K. Dick whom friends and family knew as an adult had begun to emerge. He came across as a complicated mix of awkward intellectual and suave prankster; hypersensitive to rejection because of his history of neglect and prone to react with bursts of rage; hypochondriacal; unsure of who he was and insecure in his existence; detached and alienated; and increasingly dependent on drugs, which seemed to both ameliorate and aggravate his emotional volatility. Not the sort of character, one might think, that people would enjoy being around. At the same time, Dick had a powerfully warm and creative side, and it was that aspect of his personality that could draw others to him. Before further delving into Dick's darkness, I turn next to his creativity and compassion.

4 | BEETLE SATORI

Although Dick's late life was to be defined by the mind-bending mystical experiences he had in 1974, religion was not an essential part of his childhood. While Dick's parents sent him to Sunday school, they did not identify with organized religion. Dick's father, Edgar, abandoned formal religion in revolt against the fire-and-brimstone attitude of his own parents. In Edgar's unpublished memoir, *As I Remember Them*, he portrays his family of origin as a colorful cast of Pennsylvanian religious extremists. Edgar's uncle was minister of the local church, and his Bible-quoting father, William, whipped Edgar and his siblings for the tiniest breach of discipline. Edgar recounts one incident in which he was beaten for imitating his father gargling his throat. The church was apocalyptic: once, its newsletter predicted the world was to end on a particular day, terrifying Edgar and his siblings. Edgar developed a lifelong allergy to churches. Less is known about the religious background of Dick's mother, Dorothy, although she shared Edgar's discomfort with religion. In the absence of a traditional religious context, Dick crafted his own spiritual beliefs out of his personal experiences and readings.

In his journals, Dick emphasizes several spiritual experiences from his childhood. The most striking are a Zen-like moment of illumination that happened in the third grade when he was playing with a beetle, and a voice-hearing episode caused by the anxiety of a nail-biting physics exam. Though both experiences were brief, I delve into them at length for the same reason I explored the death of Dick's sister: the importance Dick ascribes to them. Indeed, Dick declares his life's creative work can be traced to the beetle incident, a remark implying it may have had nearly as powerful an impact as the death of his twin sister. If the death of Jane was one origin story of Dick's personality, the third-grade mystical experience—which I'll call the *beetle satori*, for reasons that will become clear below—was a second origin story. Personalities are multifaceted and therefore can have several points of origin. If there is more than one tale that is so powerfully all-encompassing that it comes to define a person's identity, then it is possible for a life to have more than one origin story. Whereas the tale of Jane's death is the story of Dick's physical birth, the tale of the beetle satori is, as he tells it, the story of his spiritual birth. It is a narrative about the development of compassion.

Like many young children, Dick took pleasure in torturing insects. He says, "in third grade . . . I was tormenting a beetle. It was taking refuge in an empty snail shell. He'd come out of the snail shell and I'd mash at him with a rock, and he'd run back into the snail shell. I'd just wait until he'd come out. And he came out, and all of a sudden I realized—it was . . . just infinite, that this beetle was like I was. There was an understanding. He wanted to live just like I was, and I was hurting him. For a moment . . . I was that beetle. Immediately I was different. I was never the same again. I was totally aware of what I was doing, I was just transformed. My essence was changed." It was, Dick explains, a spiritual transformation of his identity by way of empathy.

Some might be skeptical. After all, the scenario Dick describes may not sound dramatic enough to be worthy of a spiritual interpretation. To understand why Dick thought of the beetle satori as spiritual, it helps to examine the context of religious thought in which he later placed it. Dick went back to the beetle satori repeatedly, in interviews and journals, reading and rereading it in light of several spiritual traditions. In an interview with Rickman, Dick describes it in Zen Buddhist terms as *satori* or sudden enlightenment. A guiding theme of Zen is the discovery of spiritually transcendent experiences in the mundane details of everyday life. From a Zen perspective, enlightenment can be found as readily in the act of washing dishes as in visiting a guru on a mountaintop. The chief source of Dick's knowledge of Zen was *Zen and Japanese Culture* by D. T. Suzuki. In that book, Suzuki notes the following features of a satori. Through satori, hidden meaning is revealed in mundane daily experiences. The meaning that is revealed, Suzuki says, is not superimposed on the mundane experience from thoughts or memories, but constitutes the inherent reality of the experience. For a moment, daily life becomes transparent and its inner meaning is shockingly clear. Furthermore, the meaning revealed in a satori is not abstract but concrete. Dick's revelation, similarly, was not a thought, but an immediate sensing that "this beetle was just like I was." According to Suzuki, satori is emancipatory, in that it liberates the mind from false ideas. Through immediate sensory contact, unencumbered by concepts, the meaning of existence becomes clear. Satori is a sudden sensory blast of spiritual insight.

In his journals, Dick elaborates. Switching to a Christian perspective, Dick claims that he saw the beetle "as holy, as Christ." The torment of the beetle was the Passion of Christ. Dick explains that an essential aspect of his spiritual outlook was the notion of godhood present in a dying animal, like the beetle. A vital part of the latter idea, Dick notes, is the empathic knowing of what it feels like to be the tormented animal. Let's recall that, as I discussed in the last chapter, Dick's history of trauma left him with a painful sense of detachment. The beetle satori treated his detachment by providing the emotional engagement afforded by empathy. As Dick puts it, the empathic link with the beetle breached the "prison" of his estrangement from other beings, and Dick felt connected to life. According to Dick, the empathic knowing of the suffering of the animal is given only by "the grace of God." Dick's revelation, then, was not only spiritual, but epistemological. Empathic knowing is not a rational knowing, and thus cannot be forced or reasoned out. Either you are graced with it, or you aren't. Dick considered empathic knowing to be the road to spiritual salvation. When empathy is fully realized, Dick contends, it is identical with love of God. The theory provides an antidote to loss, for if love for those we have lost is love of God, then they are "restored" to us as aspects of God.

Dick's Christian reading of his beetle satori matches the views of the theologian Pierre Teilhard de Chardin, whose book *The Phenomenon of Man* was popular in Dick's community. Teilhard, a paleontologist and Jesuit priest, made it his life's work to bridge the gap between his conflicting disciplines. Teilhard posits that even the smallest piece of matter includes a spiritual element, for otherwise, the law of entropy should have made the universe come to a halt. Accordingly, Teilhard argues, matter must have a spiritual "inner face" that drives it toward greater interconnectedness and complexity, evolving toward an Omega Point of transcendence. As humanity approaches the Omega Point, Teilhard predicts it will establish a planet-wide consciousness that Teilhard calls the *Noosphere*, borrowing the Greek term *Noos* for "mind." Teilhard conceptualizes love as the natural affinity of particles to each other. Even gravity is a form of love. Love is a force that brings the universe together, whether it pertains to people or planets. When it comes to human desire, Teilhard says every desire is a mask for the grander desire to reach spiritual fulfillment. In short, all human desires are derivatives of the love of God. From a Teilhardian perspective, then, Dick's eventual love of the beetle amounts to a love of God.

Dick's religious interpretations of the beetle satori, however, omit a psychologically intriguing feature of the experience. As Dick tells the story, he not only witnessed the torment of the beetle, but was the tormentor. It wasn't just that Dick empathized with a "dying animal," as he puts it, and that his loving empathy catalyzed a spiritual awakening. No, he empathized specifically with a dying animal *he was in the middle of killing.* His was the empathy of the torturer for the tortured, the executioner for the executed. After satori struck him, Dick says, he realized "what he was doing" and stopped. Which raises the question: what exactly *was* he doing?

Dick was playing, as I see it, a game of predatory peek-a-boo. When Dick "mashed" the beetle with the rock, it hid in the snail shell. As the beetle reappeared, Dick "mashed" at it again. Dick's attacks beat the beetle back into the shell. His account of the beetle-mashing game suggests it had a repetitive, ritualistic quality. Dick mashes, beetle hides. Dick mashes, beetle hides. If you are seen, you get mashed. If you see, you mash. Being unseen is safe. The satori occurred just as the beetle emerged from the shell, and Dick, presumably, was about to take a swing at it. His anticipation built as he waited for the beetle, and then at the climactic moment, everything transformed into empathic love. The heart of Dick's satori was "this beetle was just like I was." If so, it is important to explore precisely how the beleaguered beetle was *just like* the young Philip K. Dick. Did Dick feel like a small creature under attack by the traumas inflicted by a harsh world? Did he feel forced to psychologically retreat into a shell though depersonalization? When he emerged from his shell, did he feel repeatedly "mashed"? Dick's trauma history positioned him to identify deeply with the beetle, and therefore, it may well have been his traumatic past that set the stage for the satori. His personal suffering linked him with the suffering of other beings.

Dick does not elaborate on this aspect of his experience, but the facts are there. By the third grade, Dick had nearly starved to death because of neglect, had his twin die, had been abandoned by his father, had been sent to boarding school, and had endured multiple separations from his mother. His schoolmates attacked him with rocks, and he hid under cars to escape. Life "mashed" him hard. Perhaps Dick glimpsed a reflection of his own suffering in the torment of the beetle, and saw himself as a double of the cruel universe that had tormented *him*. The beetle was Dick, and Dick was the cruel universe. If so, when Dick stopped torturing the beetle, so too did the universe stop torturing him. Dick spared himself as he spared the beetle, loving himself as he loved the beetle. In the microcosm of his relationship with the beetle, the macrocosm of Dick's relationship with the universe was transformed. He and the cosmos were no longer at odds. They cared about each other. They could be merciful.

The core theme of the beetle satori, then, is the *sudden empathic awakening of a cruel oppressor*, leading to *an act of mercy* and *a change in attitude*. Let's call this theme the Mercy Satori. It shows up often in Dick's writings, most obviously in his oddly titled 1974 novel *Flow My Tears, The Policeman Said*, a futuristic story of identity theft. In the book, a celebrity, Jason Taverner, runs afoul of the law in a future dystopian world. Taverner awakens one morning to discover all records of his existence have vanished. His situation comes to the attention of police bureaucrats, who construe his lack of identity as grounds for suspicion. The police assume Taverner removed his records from their databases, and reason that no one but a criminal mastermind could eliminate all traces of himself. Their suspicions are literally founded on nothing. A manhunt ensues.

Later in the story, the police chief's sister dies from overdose of a drug from a police laboratory. The police chief, Felix Buckman, anticipates he might be blamed for his sister's death. Because Taverner is already under suspicion, Buckman decides to frame him to protect himself. Buckman places him under arrest, planning to have his henchmen murder Taverner and blame him for his sister's death. The titular moment of *Flow My Tears* happens after Buckman gives the order to kill Taverner and departs the police station. While commuting home, Buckman ponders Taverner's innocence and the unfairness of his circumstances. He notes that Taverner's mistake was merely in coming to the attention of the authorities—in coming to *his* attention. By making himself known, Taverner put himself in danger. Like the beetle in the beetle satori, Taverner became a target by coming out into the open. Like the young Philip Dick, Buckman was about to "mash" him.

Pondering Taverner's fate, Buckman is overwhelmed with tears. He wonders whether he is crying over his dead sister, or over Taverner. Desperate to connect with another human being, Buckman parks at a gas station and approaches a customer with a scrap of paper. On the paper, he sketches a heart with an arrow through it. The customer looks at the paper, shrugs, and hands it back. Buckman leaves, still weeping. He then impulsively returns to the gas station and embraces the customer, who asks his name. Paralyzed by guilt, Buckman replies that he "cannot bear" to remember his name, and says he has none. "I am an individual, like you," Buckman says. The customer explains that he understands Buckman's feelings, and often has similar impulses to embrace others. Comforted, Buckman regains his poise. Because of Buckman's change of attitude, he shows mercy on Taverner and lets him live.

Dick identifies *Flow My Tears* as among the most autobiographical of his books. In light of Dick's spiritual ideas, Buckman's capricious change of heart toward Taverner can be seen as a Mercy Satori. Buckman's oppression of Taverner is spiritually equivalent to the young Dick's torture of the beetle. In both scenes, a cruel tormentor on the verge of killing is transformed by a sudden flood of cosmic love leading to an act of mercy and a change in attitude. In Buckman's case, the change is so radical he temporarily loses his identity and becomes unable to utter his name. For a moment he becomes like Taverner, a man who is no one. In his journals, Dick reveals that the oppressive police state of *Tears* represents ancient Rome, as well as the oppressive establishment of the United States of 1970. *Tears* illustrates, then, how the beetle satori did not fade away with Dick's childhood, but continued to inform him well into his adult years.

Eureka

Dick's first taste of what he considered divine madness occurred during a high school physics final, which he had been told was essential for admission to college. A topic of the test was Archimedes' principle, which states that when an object is submerged, it is met with a force equal to the volume of the water that it has displaced. The story of the principle's origins may be relevant. Legend has it Archimedes was commanded to study the topic by his king, Heiro II, who needed a method to assess the volume of a crown from which he suspected his goldsmith to have stripped gold. After a long period of frustration, Archimedes is supposed to have discovered the principle when he stepped into a bathtub and, observing that the level of the water rose, famously shouted "Eureka!"

During the test, Dick, like Archimedes, was under pressure and hit a wall. Overwhelmed by performance anxiety, he forgot Archimedes' principle, which was needed to answer several items on the test. "I sat for two hours staring at the page and my college entrance depended on getting that test right. . ... I prayed and prayed and prayed and prayed and then this voice clicked on and said . . . 'the principle is really very simple'. And then it went on and stated the principle and it explained how it was applied." It was a case of miraculous rescue. Yet unlike the rescue in Dick's origin story, this rescue was not equivocal. He received a solid "A" on the test. He was saved. Eureka!

Voice hearing is not as rare as commonly believed. Contrary to popular opinion, most people who hear voices do not meet criteria for a psychiatric diagnosis. The cause of voices remains a mystery, although it has been found that voices often occur in the context of stressful or traumatic events. Voices can come when one is stranded on a mountaintop, has lost a loved one, or faces imminent death, or during similarly extreme experiences. It is consistent with what is known about voices, then, that Dick's voice-hearing experience would occur in the context of overwhelming anxiety. Although a high school physics exam might not seem like a life or death situation, anxiety is anxiety. Subjectively, Dick experienced the physics exam as a terrifying ordeal with his entire future at stake.

As Dick tells the story, his desperation and "need of an acute sort" for guidance led to a "prayer petition." Dick silently uttered a repetitious prayer, as he sat for "two hours staring at the page," mentally paralyzed. And then, after Dick's intense prayer petition, "this voice clicked on." The word "clicked" suggests a mechanical quality to the voice. Dick describes the voice as "neutral," "calm," and "female." In his later years, he would call the voice an "AI voice," perhaps like a female version of the computer Hal from *2001: A Space Odyssey*. As for the information the voice provided, Dick notes that he had carefully memorized Archimedes' principle in class, but could not access his memory. The most parsimonious explanation for the voice is that it served to bypass Dick's anxiety and access his blocked memory of Archimedes' principle.

Several characteristics of this early moment in Dick's spiritual development are striking. First, Dick was faced with massive pressure to perform. Then, under that pressure, his mind shut down, preventing him from accessing the information he needed. Faced with despair, Dick cried to the divine for help. Under the pressure of his prayer, a nonrational channel opened that allowed him to access his own intelligence. Unable to consciously remember what he knew, Dick received it as passive instruction. Dick's hallucinatory voice, then, was a linking experience that succeeded in crossing mental barriers produced by anxiety. It bridged a divide in his mind between what he knew and what he was able to apply. The voice can also be seen as the manifestation of a higher self with access to all parts of Dick's mind. It was a channel his mind used to become more whole. The theme of the hallucinated voice as avatar of psychological wholeness was to return much later in the 1970s, when Dick's life became a kind of high-pressure final exam, and his anxiety reached intolerable levels.

Voices and the Daimonic

While voices are thought of today as signs of mental impairment, prior to the eighteenth century they were believed to be a form of inspiration. In the ancient world, creativity and madness were both linked to the concept of the *daimon*, or tutelary spirit. In ancient Greece, daimons were something like spirit guides. Each person, the thinking had it, is assigned a personal daimon that watches over him or her throughout life and can provide wisdom if accessed.

Some scientists believe that hallucinated voices are the outcome of a mental process called *dissociation* rather than a symptom of severe mental illness or a religious phenomenon. Dissociation is a defensive reaction to traumatic events in which the mind protects itself from pain by walling off parts of itself. Painful memories, feelings, and even thoughts can be defensively dissociated and return as voices. In a review of the literature on hearing voices, British psychologists Longden, Badill, and Waterman found that hallucinatory voices are not necessarily related to any particular psychiatric condition, being a diagnostic feature of over fifty different mental disorders. Voice hearing also occurs in individuals who have no diagnosable psychiatric problem, and is particularly common during bereavement, sensory deprivation, hypnosis, and meditation. Ten percent to 25% of the population reports having heard a hallucinated voice at least once.

Voices, then, can be alternatively understood as products of a fractured mind, or as manifestations of a higher guiding awareness. Dick's Eureka voice was both. Because of his test anxiety, his ability to recall information was restricted. His consciousness was cut off from his fund of knowledge. By reminding Dick of mathematical knowledge he unconsciously possessed, the voice both daimonically guided him and crossed a dissociative barrier in his mind. Later we will see how the same process occurred more dramatically during some of the experiences Dick had during 2-3-74.

Creative Dissociation

In general, spiritual inspiration and creativity are often linked. The term "originality" captures some of that linkage: creativity not only *originates* new forms, but also can connect with the *origins* or sources of life itself. Historians have documented how art and religion, currently considered distinct activities, were originally inseparable. Artistic elements suffuse religious rituals. The earliest recorded works of art, cave paintings, are believed to be of religious origin. Cave paintings are thought to have provided props for shamanic initiation rituals for Paleolithic people. In ancient times, states of artistic inspiration were often equated with states of spiritual possession. The artist was an instrument in the service of supernatural forces. Throughout history, philosophers and artists have similarly linked creativity with spirituality. Dick was fond of the popular mythologist Joseph Campbell, who wrote several books depicting the crossover of religion and creativity. Campbell popularized the notion that common mythologies underlie art and religion. He introduced what he called the *monomyth*: a core story of heroic journey and accomplishment he believed to be common to all the world's mythologies. The key plot sequence of the monomyth is a departure of the hero from everyday reality into a world of adventure and risk, a series of trials and initiations, and a return into the ordinary world with a philosophical or creative insight derived from the journey. From a Campbellian perspective, Dick lived out the monomyth by leaving everyday reality in his spiritual encounters, and introducing the insights he had gleaned into ordinary life through the channel of science fiction.

One psychological view of the relationship between creativity and spirituality focuses on a *creative dissociation* through which the mind both transcends and transforms everyday reality. Clinically, dissociation is usually conceived of as a way that the mind enters a hypnotic state in order to cope with traumatic experiences by tuning them out. However, scholars have argued that dissociation also occurs in many other contexts. Both artists and mystics, according to the creative dissociation theory, share the ability to communicate with parts of the mind that are usually inaccessible. It is in dissociative states that both creative inspiration and mystical insight are received. It is likely Dick's creative and spiritual experiences were both enhanced by the facility with dissociation that Dick developed in response to trauma. As the *Exegesis* shows, Dick's creative process was an active integration of the most diverse of philosophical, scientific, and literary motifs. Everything became incorporated into Dick's writing, including the most ordinary of experiences.

Roog!

Two early Dick stories, "Roog" and "Expendable," provide simple illustrations of his creative process. Dick's process was *overincorporative*, in that his imagination consumed the details of his life and transformed them into science fiction narrative. Although many writers are inspired by real life, Dick transformed autobiography into fiction with a rare intensity. "Roog," one of the first stories Dick sold, concerns a barking dog. The dog, who believes that garbage is precious food, is alarmed when it witnesses its master's trash cans emptied into a garbage truck. Because of the dog's nonhuman perspective, it is able to detect that the garbage men are disguised predatory creatures known as "Roogs," who accept cans of garbage as a sacrifice in place of the human beings they truly wish to devour. The dog knows that, eventually, the Roogs will grow weary of the garbage, and resort to preying on the humans themselves. To alert its master, the dog exclaims "Roog! Roog!," which the neighbors mistake for barking. Yet the dog's warning goes tragically unnoticed, and the story ends as it desperately shouts at the fleeing Roogs.

The origin of the story illustrates central features of Dick's creative process. "Roog" was inspired by a real-life neighbor's dog who often woke Dick from sleep by barking at garbage men. Dick took the real dog and wove it into his story. Examine the sequence. First, Dick's natural process of sleep was interrupted by a banal aspect of everyday reality: a barking dog. Second, the inspiration happened halfway between sleep and waking. Dick was later to experiment with induced hypnagogic states, dissociated mental states between sleep and waking in which visions and inspirations can occur. Third, the disruption was caused by the discrepant perspective of another mind and agenda intruding on Dick's own—in this case, the mind of the barking dog. Fourth, Dick protected his process by appropriating the impinging mind into his own creative work. The dog wouldn't let him dream, so he "dreamed" *it* by writing it into his story. Fifth, Dick's version of creative assimilation was *heavily personalized*, a kind of aggressive terraforming of reality into the shape of his own imagination. As a result of Dick's creative assimilation of impinging reality elements, his art became larger than life. Each impingement, each intrusion on his world, was transformed into an opportunity for creative expansion. Everything was material.

Bugged

Another popular early Dick story, "Expendable," provides another pointed illustration of Dick's overincorporative creative process. Dick writes that he got the idea for the story when a fly buzzed near his head and he had the thought that the fly was looking at him. In "Expendable," an unnamed man leaves his house one day to notice two caterpillars talking about him. "There he goes . . . send in your report," one says. The story then portrays an army of ants plotting an attack against him. When the man returns home that night, a spider warns him that he is in danger. When he enters his house, a mass of ants comes at him and he uses his garden hose to spray them away. Later, a spider informs him that ants originally ruled the Earth until it was invaded by humans, who were originally of extraterrestrial origin. Spiders were bred by humans to protect them from the ants. Spiders may be able to save humanity from the ants, a spider tells the protagonist, but they cannot save him. The story cuts out as the floor of the house begins to heave and give way to an upsurge of invading ants.

Once again, notice how Dick's creativity works by elaborating on an experience of impingement. Dick's inspiration begins when he is interrupted by the impinging stimulus of a fly buzzing near his head. Most of us would brush off that annoyance, just as we would brush off the aggravation of being awoken in the night by a barking dog. Dick's mind, though, took minor annoyances in a different direction. As with the barking dog, Dick takes the perspective of the ant and elaborates a universe of the imagination based on that perspective. In "Roog," the imaginary universe springs from his vision of how the world might appear from the viewpoint of the barking dog. In "Expendable," the imaginary universe similarly emerges from Dick's fantasy of how the fly might see things. Different perspectives breed different worlds. Through his creative appropriation of the fly's perspective, Dick used it to breed a world of his own.

Because Dick's creative process incorporated impinging realities into his imagination, it would make sense that the greater the impingement, the greater the incorporation. The more a stressful reality intruded into Dick's world, in other words, the more powerfully he had to transform it into fiction. Understanding this aspect of Dick's creative process is one of several keys to understanding 2-3-74. 2-3-74 occurred during a period in Dick's life in which everyday reality became overwhelmingly impinging. As I will discuss later, Dick was hounded by the IRS, had a new baby, and was reeling from the recent death of a friend. The self-created world of his life was under massive intrusion from outside forces. His creativity responded to an intrusive reality by swallowing it whole. The encroaching environment became ancient Rome, frightening letters became secret messages, and Dick was transformed from an impoverished sci-fi writer into a religious revolutionary. In a sense, 2-3-74 was Dick's greatest work of science fiction. It was a creative transformation of reality itself.

The Cracks Where the Light Shines In

In sum, we can now list three psychospiritual abilities Dick developed because of his history of trauma. His experiences of being "mashed" by neglect and cruelty allowed him to empathize with the suffering of all living beings. To cope with anxiety, his mind learned to defensively dissociate, a coping strategy that prepared Dick to enter the altered states of consciousness during which experiences like voice hearing can occur. Not only did Dick dissociate in response to stress, but he also creatively incorporated impinging events into the world of his imagination. He developed the capacity for *mystical oneness*, for accessing higher parts of his mind through *dissociation*, and for *imaginatively reshaping reality*. By transforming trauma into these abilities, Dick placed himself on a developmental trajectory that had the potential to lead him to mystical states of mind.

5 | DOUBLE

In a passage from his journals, Dick writes that all of his stories are aspects of a larger narrative about the inbreaking of a forgotten real world into an illusory world. In the classic Philip K. Dick story, the protagonist notices minute discrepancies in the structure of reality that eventually reveal that it is false. The parties responsible for the spurious world vary from one story to another: depending on which tale one reads, the illusion may have been created by aliens, computers, hallucinogenic drugs, or simply malaise. However, the basic theme remains the same. The protagonist's world is exposed as a fake, and an underlying reality resurfaces. What had appeared real is revealed to be reality's double.

One aspect of Dick's grand narrative is the rediscovery of a forgotten self. In a sort of hide-and-seek game of identity, the true self is lost, replaced by a simulacrum that is eventually exposed as false. In the short story "Imposter," a man named Spence Olham is accused of being an android from Alpha Centauri deployed to destroy the Earth. His accusers inform him that the real Spence Olham was murdered and he is an android imposter. They tell him that his body houses a bomb rigged to explode and destroy the planet when activated by a key phrase. The indignant Olham tries to prove he is the real thing, only to discover at the end of the story that he is, indeed, an android. Finding the corpse of the real Spence Olham, he exclaims "But if that's Olham, then I must be—" As this phrase is uttered, the bomb goes off and destroys the Earth.

"Imposter" offers a different perspective than typical stories of self-discovery. Classic stories about self-discovery portray knowledge of self as a catalyst for a better life. When Dickens' Oliver Twist realizes his true identity, he discovers he is heir to a fortune. Dick's Spence Olham, by contrast, blows up and takes the whole world with him. "Imposter" suggests that it may be preferable never to learn who one really is. In memoirs, Dick writes of a recurrent dream of searching through piles of magazines for a terrifying story he does not want to find. Like Dick in his dream, Olham is inexorably driven to uncover a secret that will prove to be his own destruction. Self-awareness, "Imposter" has it, can be explosive. The truth destroys.

What kills Olham is not only the unmasking of his false identity, but the revelation that he is a destructive entity. It is bad enough to realize that one is not oneself, but to discover that one is actually a soulless instrument of evil is tough to top on the scale of hard truths. Part of the problem is that if one were to make such a discovery, one would be forced to *become* a soulless instrument of evil in order to be true to oneself. Nietzsche famously advised: "Become what you are." Dick's thought-provoking reply: But what if what you are is evil? Should you follow Nietzsche's advice if it means destroying yourself, your loved ones, and the entire planet Earth?

There is psychological sense to be made of Dick's troubling tale. Dick was familiar with C. G. Jung's concept of the psychological shadow. Jung postulates that most people identify excessively with their persona, the socially acceptable face they present to others. They become the people that social convention demands they be. Identification with the persona carries a high price for, in order to conform to it, one must dissociate aspects of the personality that are socially unacceptable. To fit the image I want to present to others, I have to forget about the parts of myself that conflict with it. These erased parts of the personality, Jung claims, coalesce into a dark alter ego: the shadow. According to Jung, the shadow takes on a life of its own as a second self that sabotages a person's conscious goals. Often, the shadow is projected onto others, who are then perceived as threatening. In Jung's view, projection has a boomerang effect: the parts of yourself you push away come back at you from the outside. As Jung puts it, "Everything that irritates us about others can lead us to an understanding of ourselves."

The psychoanalyst Otto Rank makes a similar argument in a classic study of doubles entitled, simply, *Double*. Rank's reading of the double aligns with Jung's conception of the shadow, but takes the psychoanalytic line of thinking a step further. Rank points out that in literature the doppelganger not only represents denied parts of the self (as it does for Jung) but also permits the protagonist to satisfy forbidden wishes without guilt. Take Dr. Jekyll and Mr. Hyde: Mr. Hyde lives out the dark urges that Jekyll forbids himself. From Rank's angle, Dick's android double permits the human to freely live out his or her darker impulses. Olham's android does what Olham could not: he destroys the world.

Jung's and Rank's ideas about doubles highlight a central theme running through Dick's life and stories: the contradiction between who Dick liked to think he was, and who he *feared* he was. This chapter is devoted to that contradiction, the difference between Dick and his shadow. Consistent with his spiritual beliefs, Dick's persona was of compassion. In a letter to his wife Anne, he writes, "My image of myself is this gentle saint-like sage." Informed by the theme of the Mercy Satori described in the previous chapter, Dick romanticized empathy and kindness toward animals. In accord with his ideals, he saw himself as a rescuer who took on the most desperate cases among his acquaintances. Friends were captivated by his warmth and generosity. Yet, stories like "Imposter" express his fear that deep inside, he was a destructive entity. As I describe later, in the 1970's the narrative hints of Dick's unconscious explosiveness gave way to a full-blown delusion that he was brainwashed and programmed to self-destruct. Dick's terror became so overwhelming that he called the police and warned them he was a machine and should be incarcerated. Dick *was* Spence Olham, and Olham was Dick.

Like Olham, Dick was explosive. As mentioned in the last chapter, he had temper tantrums since early childhood. Often, they occurred when his mother was unavailable. Although it is common for young children to react to separations with tantrums, most children outgrow them. Dick did not. When he grew up, his tantrums grew up with him, becoming episodes of violent rage. Dick rarely acknowledged his outbursts and often could not remember them. In a letter written in 1972, Dick confesses to a "primary hostility." "I am mad at everyone and everything," he writes.

It makes sense that Dick rarely recalled his rage attacks. As Jung and many others have noted, it is common for explosive outbursts to occur in dissociated states of mind. Sometimes, these outbursts are related to a history of trauma. Trauma survivors often dissociate when they encounter situations that activate flashbacks of traumatic events. When a flashback is triggered, the traumatized person perceives the world as dangerous or even hostile. Sometimes, a person in a flashback may counterattack against the hostility that he or she mistakenly perceives in the environment. From the perspective of those witnessing such a dissociative event, the trauma trigger is often invisible and the explosive outburst looks irrational. Before, I wrote of Dick's infamous attempt to swerve his car into oncoming traffic when his girlfriend, Linda Levy, said she would be spending the evening with another science fiction writer, Norman Spinrad, rather than with him. I would conjecture that when Levy informed Dick of her plan to spend the evening with Spinrad instead of Dick, her remark tripped off a flashback of Dick's abandonment traumas. At that fraught moment, Levy's words opened a psychological time portal that returned Dick to his childhood. To Levy, the time was the 1970s. To Dick, it was the 1930s and he was being abandoned by his mother all over again. Death at Levy's side must have seemed preferable. At least that way, he wouldn't have to be alone.

Some of Dick's theoretical essays address topics associated with his shadow. In "Man, Android, and Machine," Dick writes of "fierce cold things" that masquerade as humans by imitating human behavior. He calls these fierce doubles *androids*. In this essay, Dick does not use the word *androids* to refer to the robots of science fiction. Rather, he means to describe real people who operate in an inhumane and robotlike fashion. Human androids are identifiable by their lack of empathy for others. They wear the masks of humans, but are uncaring underneath. What makes a person human or android, Dick argues, is not whether that person is made of metal or flesh but whether his or her makeup includes compassion. In writing "Man, Android, and Machine," Dick had in mind the manipulative behavior of drug addicts and psychopaths. However, because he wrote the essay just after a severe struggle with his own addiction, it also may well allude to his own conflicted personality.

In another essay, "The Android and the Human," Dick elaborates. Human beings and machines, he writes, are increasingly difficult to distinguish. As technology advances, computers become more like human minds. Further, Dick says, our dehumanizing society treats human beings as instruments used as means to an end. Given the increasing resemblance of machine and human, Dick suggests, it is vital to identify the behavior that is unique to humans so that we can tell the difference between ourselves and our machines. To clarify these differences, Dick describes two problematic features of the android mind. For one thing, the android mechanically repeats the same behavior even when it achieves no positive result. Its actions are predictable and repetitious, because the android cannot make exceptions. It deals with every situation identically. Second, the android approaches life through thought rather than feeling. The android *reifies* itself and others, coldly treating people as things rather than human beings.

These characteristics of the android are Dick's shadow side, writ large. Like the androids he feared, Dick often assumed a cerebral approach toward life. Ursula Le Guin called him a calculating "computer." Dick's third wife, Anne, said Dick "had this enormous gift of empathy, and he used it to woo and please and control . . . He just had a very dark shadow." Anne's remark is telling.

Although Dick had deep empathy for others, he sometimes used it to charm rather than to help. Despite his enormous capacity for love, he often approached conflict with his loved ones by scheming and calculating. As for Dick's violence, it, like the android, was repetitive. It occurred nearly across the board in his close relationships with women, a response to traumatic memories rather than to these women as individuals. Dick was an android, a deadly double of himself. His android theorizing was covert autobiography.

The Android Femme Fatale

Dick confessed he was filled with rage toward his mother for neglect, and biographers conjecture he vented that rage on the women to whom he was closest. From this perspective, Dick's romantic partners, like Linda Levy, were mother figures that Dick unconsciously used as targets of his anger towards his mother for her early neglect. In psychological theory, Dick's pattern in relationships would be thought of as *transference*. According to research, a person's formative relationships in childhood give rise to preconceived expectations of how future relationships will unfold. Studies show, for example, that adults tend to select romantic partners who resemble their parents. Adults *transfer* childhood feelings associated with parental figures onto significant others. We learn how to love from our families of origin. We see our lovers, our boyfriends and girlfriends, wives and husbands, through the lens of early experiences with parents. When we are in the grip of transference, we do not perceive a romantic partner as a unique individual, but rather as one edition in a series of love objects that stretches all the way back to infanthood. As Freud famously said, every finding of a love object is a refinding.

Transference also informs the creative process. It's been noted that Dick's female characters are often villainous. Many are cruel seductresses, and some are androids. In *Do Androids Dream of Electric Sheep?* a bounty hunter named Rick Deckard is assigned to kill a gang of androids who illegally immigrated to Earth from outer space. To track down the androids, Deckard enlists the help of Rachel Rosen, the daughter of the androids' creator. In a twist, Rosen is revealed to be an android herself. Unbeknownst to Deckard, she is a secret ally of the androids he was tasked to destroy. Rosen seduces Deckard, hoping to make him empathize with androids like her so that he will spare her android friends. She plans to use the very quality that separates human from android—empathy—against Deckard. However, the betrayed Deckard destroys the rogue androids, and Rosen takes revenge by killing his pet goat.

Malevolent characters like Rosen can be thought of as transferential figures expressing Dick's conflicted feelings toward women. Even when Dick's fictional women don't turn out to be androids, they are often dangerous. In *Ubik*, a telepathic femme fatale seduces the protagonist, Joe Chip. Chip notices that she has a tattoo of the phrase "caveat emptor" (buyer beware). In *A Scanner Darkly*, the protagonist, Bob Arctor, develops a relationship with Donna Hawthorne, a drug dealer. Hawthorne is an undercover agent who manipulates Arctor into excessive drug use, resulting in brain damage. In *Clans of the Alphane Moon*, Dick portrays a marriage that has gone so sour that the husband and wife, Chuck and Mary Rittersdorf, try to assassinate each other. The message of these books is clear: from Dick's perspective, women are hazardous. They have ulterior motives, they try to kill you, and they may not even be human. Watch out.

A Homicidal Marriage: Anne and Philip

Two Dick scholars, Christopher Palmer and Umberto Rossi, argue that the homicidal marriage of Chuck and Mary Rittersdorf was a fictionalized portrait of Dick's own marriage to his third wife, Anne Rubinstein, in the early 1960s. Dick's first marriage was with Jeanette Marlin, a customer at a record store where he worked as a young adult. Their union was impulsive and brief, lasting only six months in 1948. A year and a half later, Dick was smitten with another customer, Kleo Apostolides, who shared his musical and philosophical interests. Dick and Apostolides married in 1950, and their relationship was stable enough to endure for about 10 years. It began to falter in 1958 when the couple moved to Point Reyes, California, and Dick met Anne Rubinstein.

Anne's husband had died just two weeks before she met Dick, and he had bequeathed to her a large farmhouse in Point Reyes, a modest inheritance, and three daughters. Lonely and curious, Anne paid Philip a welcome visit. The two were immediately lovestruck, and two weeks later Philip declared his love for Anne. He exclaimed that she represented everything he ever dreamed of.

In Chapter 3, I noted that Philip's history of trauma and neglect contributed to *depersonalization*, a painful sense of detachment. Philip's letters to Anne indicate that the intense passion of their relationship was successful, at least temporarily, in dissolving the psychological barriers that kept Philip detached from life. Love was an antidote to depersonalization. In one 1958 letter, for example, he dramatizes a phone call from Anne that healed a sense of separation from her and from the world. "Then when you called . . . distance was abolished, and the return of you as a physical reality caused a genuine transformation in me, as if I had stepped from one world to another . . . There is a direct relationship between my hearing you, and the religious person who, after the traditional isolation and fasting and meditation, 'hears' the voice of 'god'." Philip's love for Anne was a blockbusting religious experience, transforming him and sweeping him into another world. "In a sense," he writes, "I did undergo [religious] conversion upon hearing from you." Some women would have fled, detecting danger in Philip's all-consuming passion. Anne didn't. Philip divorced Kleo and moved in with Anne, and the lovers married on April Fool's Day.

For Philip, the marriage was a transferential perfect storm. It seemed to promise a love cure for his existential pain, only to exacerbate it. Part of how ecstatic love works is that it tends to open one's wounds along with one's heart, offering the potential for both healing and harm. Oblivious to Philip's sensitivities, Anne conflated Philip with her deceased husband, introducing him to friends as "Richard." Then, she laughed it off, joking "one husband is the same as another." For a man who had from early childhood been told by his mother that he should have died instead of his twin sister, being substituted for a dead man by his beloved wife must have been disturbing. Philip's marriage to Anne touched on all his sore spots. Like Philip's mother, Anne was an intellectual with an acerbic wit. Like Philip's mother,

Anne conflated him with a deceased loved one she had never fully mourned.

Trauma survivors are often unwittingly attracted to situations that resemble their core traumas. They re-enact traumatizing experiences to gain a feeling of control. If Philip could thrive in a marriage to a woman like his mother, a powerful woman who felt him to be a substitute for a dead loved one, he might prove that he was not damaged by his mother after all. Not only would his emotional wounds be healed in the present, but his past would be retroactively healed as well. It was an attempt at a do-over. Philip's need to reshape his early traumas explains why, when his and Anne's daughter was born, he cryptically said, "Now my sister is made up for."

As time went on, the destructive side of the marriage began to outweigh its therapeutic benefit. The two triggered each other. Philip blasted Anne with anger, eliciting her own tendency to escalate when angry. The couple bickered frequently. Philip dropped bombs like "I had a perfectly good wife that I traded in for you," perhaps in retaliation for feeling like a replacement of Anne's deceased husband. Anne recounts one incident in 1963 when Philip drove their car off the road and parked it halfway over a mountainside. He tried to pull her into the driver's seat, telling her "Get in and I'll push." The front of the car was pointed over a cliff. In Anne's memoir, she writes that their fights came from "no identifiable source." I would add that the source of their fights was not consciously identifiable because it had its roots in Philip's painful past.

Another factor contributing to Philip's irritability was his consumption of amphetamines. During his marriage to Anne, he secretly wolfed down increasingly massive doses to fuel the frenetic pace of his writing. Amphetamines act on several neurotransmitters, most prominently dopamine, which is related to pleasure and emotion regulation. Speed floods the user's brain with dopamine, providing an exhilarating experience of confident happiness. In the long term, though, the brain adapts to the dopamine flooding by becoming desensitized to it. As a result, it becomes increasingly difficult for an amphetamine addict to feel good, both while using and while sober. Because amphetamine abuse erodes the brain's ability to generate pleasure, it increases anxiety and aggression.

Over time, amphetamine abuse often leads to amphetamine-induced psychotic disorder, a condition in which hallucinations and paranoid delusions occur. People with amphetamine-induced paranoia are hyperalert to small aspects of the environment that seem out of place, and fill these with significance. They monitor with minute scrutiny the smallest variations in the behavior of other people and can construe these as evidence of malicious intent. Consistent with his amphetamine paranoia, Philip accused Anne of plotting to murder him. Once, Anne relates, she and Philip were driving around their farm, and Philip exited the car to open a gate. Anne edged the car slightly forward and Philip fled in terror, apparently in the belief that Anne intended to run him over.

Although Dick's paranoia was drug-induced, all paranoia also has a psychological dimension. Psychologically, paranoia is characterized by projection. Projection is a defense mechanism in which the mind attributes unacceptable qualities of oneself to another person, in order to distance oneself from them. For example, paranoid people uncomfortable with sexual feelings accuse others of inappropriate sexual overtures, and those who struggle with hostility perceive it everywhere but themselves. Philip fell within the latter category. Recall Jung's ideas about the shadow: it is often disowned and attributed to other people. Dick's addiction fed his shadow, and it grew larger and more dangerous.

Aggravating these problems, any severe addiction causes a split personality. The addicted self may be unrecognizable to friends and family. At one moment, the addict may appear rational, only to be overcome by irrational drug-fueled behavior. It is probably no coincidence that during his time with Anne, Philip had several doppelganger experiences. He told Anne that he walked into the living room and found a double of himself standing there. He had encountered his future self, apparently having already reached his destination. Later, while lying on the bed, Philip witnessed a double getting dressed. His perspective suddenly shifted, and he observed himself lying on the bed from the point of view of the double. The experience of hallucinating a double of one's own body is called *autoscopy*, and it can occur in a variety of altered states of consciousness, including drug intoxication and the twilight states between sleep and waking. It also has a literary meaning: autoscopy is reputed to be a sign that one's death is imminent. For instance, Abraham Lincoln is famously believed to have seen a double image of his face in the weeks before his assassination. During his time with Anne, Philip read a biography of Lincoln by Carl Sandburg that referenced Lincoln's deadly double.

Anne was struck by the duality in Philip's own attitude towards their relationship. On the one hand, Philip worked hard to be "the perfect husband," as Anne put it. He charmed Anne and played sensitively with her children. He was genuinely loving.

On the other hand, Philip communicated rage and terror. He composed stories about homicidal women, and slipped hurtful remarks into conversations. A friend, Maury Guy, reports that Philip's complaints were usually some version of "Anne's marvelous, she's terrible, she's marvelous and she's getting more terrible by the moment." A neighbor, June Kresy, says that Philip ran to her in fear and exclaimed he was terrified of Anne. Philip's Hugo Award–winning novel *The Man in the High Castle* is prefaced by the hostile dedication: "To my wife, Anne, without whose silence this book would never have been written." A female character in the novel, Juliana Frink, is based on Anne. Frink is a judo instructor who develops a sexual relationship with an assassin and kills him, slashing his throat.

Henry Krystal, an authority on addiction, observes that many addicts were neglected children, and grow up believing they have no right to care for themselves. Accordingly, they place responsibility for their self-care outside themselves, onto substances and other people. By disclaiming personal ownership over self-care, addicts blur boundaries between self and other. The addict can feel as if uncomfortable feelings come from others, rather than the self. In Krystal's view, when addicts feel distress they automatically have thoughts of rejection or punishment by loved ones. From the addict's perspective, when feelings are unpleasant, others are to blame. Because of that logic, addicts often react to painful emotions by attacking those closest to them.

Krystal's ideas jibe with what is known about the dynamic between Anne and Philip, which became ever more volatile. Philip threw furniture and hit Anne. Using his considerable powers of persuasion, he convinced friends and family that it was Anne, not he, who was abusive. No doubt Philip was able to make a good case, because he genuinely felt he was the victim. He told his psychiatrist Anne had tried to run him over with a car, threatened him with a knife, and planned to mortgage the house to buy a record business. (The record business was actually Philip's idea.) His psychiatrist believed the story and arranged for Anne to be committed to a psychiatric hospital. Philip had reshaped reality to match his projections. It was *Philip* who was psychotic, but he used his knowledge of psychiatry to convince his doctor that *Anne* was mad. The mental health laws of that time gave little support to patients' rights, and Anne was locked up for several weeks. On her release, Anne was prescribed Stelazine, an antipsychotic drug with severe side effects. There is no evidence that Anne was ever psychotic. Philip threatened to leave Anne if she did not take the medication.

Anne's psychiatric commitment was the beginning of the end of the marriage. Philip's physical abusiveness escalated. In the heat of arguments, his fists flew. Then, he embraced Anne tightly and sobbed. Childlike rage toward Anne alternated with abject dependence. I would guess that after Philip had expressed his rage, he was terrified Anne would abandon him and grabbed her tight to make sure she did not leave. The attacks continued for some time. Anne says Philip only stopped when she raised her own fists and advanced on him. He retreated in terror. He told a friend, Inez Storer, that he could not live with or without Anne and would kill himself because of her. Finally, in June 1964, Philip filed for divorce. Anne's attorney was to tell her, years later, that the divorce case was the most difficult of her career.

As the divorce was finalized, Dick moved to Oakland to live with Grania Davis, a fan who had sent flirtatious letters. It did not take him long to transform his relationship with Davis into a death trip. Soon after the move, he attempted suicide by running his VW Beetle off the road while Davis was a passenger. Davis survived unscathed, but Dick was seriously injured and in a body cast for several months. He complained he was such a failure that he had failed even at suicide. He added that he was now spiritually dead, a "human corpse." In a story published a few years later entitled "A Little Something for Us Tempunauts," Dick writes of a group of time travelers stuck in a repeating loop of time. The group is present at their own funerals, and ride in a parade standing over their own coffins. Realizing that they are stuck in a circle, one of the time travelers, Addison, proposes to bring a dangerously large amount of mass with him into the time machine. The group hopes that it will cause an explosion and end the loop. In the story, Addison's girlfriend assists him by bringing him a box full of old VW Beetle parts, which he takes with him through time. However, it turns out that the explosion does not end the loop, but recreates it. Had Dick hoped that suicide via Volkswagen might free him from the vicious cycle in which he was trapped?

Dick continued to have persecutory delusions about Anne. As the amphetamine abuse grew, so did Dick's paranoia. He complained that Anne used his record player as a microphone to monitor him, and that she broke into his office and stole his financial papers. In amphetamine psychosis, delusions of being monitored and burgled are commonplace. Dick was so terrified of Anne he bought a pistol to defend himself. When she visited him in Oakland, he waved the gun at her, scaring her away. Regarding the gun waving, think projection: did she want to kill Dick or did *he* want to kill *her*? The next time Anne visited, he forced Davis to hide in the closet while they had tea. He told her everyone around him must be crazy, "or they wouldn't be closely involved with Philip K. Dick." Taking the hint, Davis left him on Halloween of 1964.

Bishop Pike

In 1964 Dick made a new friend: the celebrated Episcopal bishop James Pike, who is considered one of Dick's great mentors. Pike's views were notoriously controversial. He challenged basic Christian doctrines including hell, original sin, the holy trinity, and the virginity of Mary. He also advocated for the acceptance of LGBT individuals into the church. Pike's style was to modernize Christianity in unconventional ways. For example, at Grace Cathedral in San Francisco, he tried to install a stained glass window depicting the astronaut John Glenn as one of the saints. Pike's views were so radical that he was censured by the church for heresy. Like Dick, Pike was a personality divided. Despite his accomplishments, he was a polarizing figure whose weaknesses included alcoholism and romantic scandal. Dick first met Pike because he was having an affair with Maren Hackett, whom Dick knew through his church.

Pike's eldest son Jim Jr. committed suicide in 1966. Devastated, Pike turned to the occult, attempting to reach his son through séances. Dick was present at one such event as transcriber, and claimed to have a vision of Jim Jr. Little is known about the conversations between Pike and Dick, although it is clear Pike's heretical theology was a tremendous influence on Dick and that he identified with Pike's unconventional intellectuality. To Dick, Pike was a better self, a benign double. Once, Dick had a dream in which he was Pike. Several years later, in 1969, Pike was to die of exposure in the Israeli desert in search of information about the historical Jesus. Dick was devastated. During 2-3-74, Dick felt guided by Pike's spirit. He believed that like Pike's son in the séances, Pike himself was "coming through from the Other Side."

Nancy Hackett and the Wild Years

After Grania, Dick dated a 21-year-old woman named Nancy Hackett, stepdaughter of James Pike's lover Maren Hackett. Hackett's biological mother died of a brain tumor when she was a teenager, so like Dick, she was a child of loss. Her father was an alcoholic who is said to have been both volatile and charming, much like Dick. During Dick's periods of relative stability, she saw him as a protective figure who accepted her as she was, a "real rescuer" as she put it. Another connection between the two was that they shared several of the same phobias. Nevertheless, there was a substantial age difference. Writing the novel *Counter-Clock World*, Dick used Nancy Hackett as inspiration for a character named Lotta, who is married to a man so old he has died and been resurrected. In the novel, time runs backward. The dead are reborn, authors are paid for their books to be destroyed rather than published, and humans ingest feces and defecate food. Friends noted that similarly, Hackett's relationship to Dick seemed backward. He wrote in a letter that he felt like he had ended up in the wrong universe. Dick called Hackett his "consort," and told a friend he was worried that because he loved her too much, eventually she would "break" him. Dick pursued Hackett ardently, and they were married in 1966 after she became pregnant. Pike blessed the couple at the wedding. It must have been an awkward ceremony, as Pike was still engaged in his love affair with Hackett's stepmother.

In an interview, Dick said he knew the marriage was doomed from the start. Hackett, in turn, saw him as "a man beset by fears and insecurity." According to her, Dick was "hyper" because of amphetamines. She reports that during their relationship, Dick took up to seventy pills a day, including Valium, tranquilizers, and antipsychotic medications, as well as his ever-expanding regimen of amphetamines. Not only did Dick purchase speed from drug dealers, but he also saw several different doctors and manipulated them into prescribing the drugs he wanted by feigning symptoms of various illnesses. Again, Dick was playing the character of *Mandrake the Magician*, using illusion to achieve his ends. In the addiction field, two-timing one's doctors is known as "double dipping," a hallmark of severe addiction. Dick's drug-enhanced anxieties multiplied. He avoided driving and going outdoors. Nevertheless, drugs provided an irresistible boost to his writing. With chemical assistance, he wrote nonstop for days at a time, immersing himself so deeply in his stories that he lost track of where he was, emerging from his study in a state of disorientation. He tried and failed to quit amphetamines several times.

In 1966, Dick wrote three novels: *Do Androids Dream of Electric Sheep?*, *Ubik*, and *A Maze of Death*. Each features characters desperate to be saved from death. In all of them, the longed-for rescue appears, but equivocally. In *Do Androids Dream*, characters seek redemption through their savior Mercer, who is able to resurrect the dead. At a crucial moment in the story, Mercer appears and saves the protagonist, Rick Deckard, from being shot. Later, Deckard is overjoyed to find a toad, considered a sacred animal to Mercer. However, the toad turns out to be a fake, which places the reality of Mercer himself into question. In *Ubik*, several agents are gravely injured after undertaking a dangerous mission for their boss, Runciter. Their bodies are cryogenically frozen, but their minds remain active within a telepathically shared mental world. They have repeated experiences in which Runciter appears, sending them aid. However, at the end of the story, no one is able to leave the dying world, and only one character survives. In *A Maze of Death*, a group of people are trapped in a spaceship stuck in orbit around a dead star. To pass the time, they participate in a computer-generated virtual reality in which the deities of their respective religions answer their most fervent prayers. One of the space travelers, Seth Morley, is overcome by hopelessness and plans suicide. Before he can kill himself, Morley is rescued from the spaceship by a deity from the computer program. Has Morley been rescued, or has he merely been deceived by another layer of the virtual-reality simulation? A psychological reading of these novels might go like this: Dick felt helplessly trapped in a reality that was killing him. He was desperate for rescue, but lacked faith that it would come.

Irvin Yalom, an expert on death anxiety, studied how terminal cancer patients cope with the knowledge of their impending death. Yalom contends that fear of death is a fundamental human anxiety, and that most people respond to it with two self-deceptions: first, an irrational belief that our own specialness will exempt us from death, and, second, the equally irrational belief that if we merge with a powerful figure we will be rescued from death. The latter defensive belief, which Yalom terms *the defense of the ultimate rescuer*, is based on formative experiences with primary caregivers. According to Yalom, early experiences of being parented fuel religious hopes of being rescued by a parentlike deity. Given Dick's childhood experiences of inconsistent parenting, it makes sense that he would both long for a savior and mistrust that savior. Were Dick's parents truly there for him? Was Runciter? Was Mercer? Or did these figures promise loving protection only to disappear when it was most needed? In the face of danger, could anyone be trusted to help?

With the help of Dick's parents, he and Hackett bought a house in San Venetia in 1967. Hackett gave birth to a daughter in March and they named her Isolde Freya. Dick wrote that he had a "tendency to hate babies" because of the "competition" for his wife's attention. In addition, his childhood anxieties about nourishment resurfaced. Dick tried to make Isolde swallow too much milk, and she stopped drinking it. Adding to the stress, Hackett's mother committed suicide in June of 1967. Dick was overwhelmed. In a letter to his friend Carol Carr, he writes of a half-day–long bout of psychosis in which he

"Saw [his and Hackett's] baby as a horrid vegetable—pulpy, like a mushroom growing up, and then sinking back, again and again. Vivid horrible tastes and pain of a trigeminal sort, inability to spell words or to type. Loss of memory . . . Had

Nancy hide my gun. Bees in head. Helplessness. I couldn't cross the room . . . Delusion was that an alien outside force was controlling my mind and directing me to commit suicide . . . Acute terror while feeding the baby."

Dick couldn't bear to be alone, and demanded that Nancy be available to him 24 hours a day.

The stresses of that period, aggravated by drug abuse, awakened Dick's childhood feelings about his twin sister. It is likely Dick was terrified of feeding his baby because he feared that he, like his mother, would fail to provide proper nourishment and the baby would die, like his twin sister. His overfeeding of Isolde was overcompensation for that fear. At the same time, Dick wanted to win the "competition" for his wife's love. When the danger of emotional starvation looms, there is no room to share. It fits, then, that Dick felt hostility toward the baby as competitor. Perhaps the delusional force pushing Dick to suicide was a psychological echo of his mother's wish that he had died instead of his sister, but switched to the future tense rather than the past tense. Rather than Isolde dying, Dick should die.

As Dick deteriorated, the roles in his relationship reversed. Hackett became the adult while Dick regressed into a childlike state. When Hackett left the house, he demanded that she call to check on him. He required constant attention. Old friends said Dick no longer seemed like the man they knew. Given the role reversal, one can see even more clearly why Dick felt Isolde was a competitor. He had pulled Hackett into a maternal role while he took the role of the infant. As in *Counter-Clock World,* Dick had reversed the flow of time and recreated his own childhood with Hackett. Perhaps, as with Anne, he hoped he could make his childhood come out right this time.

Nevertheless, Dick was plagued by adult problems. The IRS audited him relentlessly, hounding him for tens of thousands of dollars of back taxes throughout the late 1960s and early 1970s. In 1968, Dick signed a War Tax Protest pledge affirming that signers would withhold tax payments in opposition to the Vietnam War. The pledge appeared as an ad in three publications. In 1969, the IRS seized Dick's car.

A story written in 1967 entitled "Faith of Our Fathers" takes place in a future world dominated by Communist China. The protagonist, Chien, buys a package of snuff containing an anti-psychotic drug. Inhaling it while watching a television broadcast of a speech by the leader of the Communist Party, Chien perceives him as a squawking robot. He meets the leader and discovers he is an evil god who preys on the energy of living things. Maybe Dick had the IRS in mind. After writing "Faith of Our Fathers," he worried that there was more truth in it than he realized and that he had unwittingly disclosed a government secret.

One of Dick's most acclaimed stories, "The Electric Ant," written in 1968, has a related theme. In it, Garson Poole, director of an electronics company, is hospitalized after an injury. To his surprise, his doctors reveal that he is an android. Examining his circuitry, Poole discovers a spool of tape responsible for filtering his subjective perception of reality. Holes punched in the tape allow bits of reality to shine through. Poole decides that if he cuts the tape entirely, he will be able to perceive all of reality at once, without filters. Poole's secretary, watching him experiment on himself, warns he is attempting suicide. Poole concurs. He cuts the tape, has an overwhelming experience of multiple realities at once, and dies. His secretary, who was merely a stimulus on his reality tape, fades away as well.

"Faith of Our Fathers" and "The Electric Ant" convey some of the psychological purposes of Dick's drug use. Leon Wurmser, who developed influential theories on addiction, suggests that a chief motivation to use drugs is control over one's state of consciousness. Contrary to popular belief, drug use is about not only the pleasure of getting high, but mastery of one's inner world. As Wurmser puts it, "drugs provide a sense of magical domination and manipulation over one's inner life, analogous to that which science and technology appear to have over the outside." Wurmser's formulation is "The Electric Ant" in summary. Psychoactive drugs are technology turned inward, and as such, treat the self as a mechanism to be recalibrated. In Wurmser's view, each drug user is a Garson Poole, punching holes in the reality tape of his or her consciousness at the risk of damaging its inner workings. Wurmser argues that each psychoactive drug is used to protect the addict against specific painful feelings. He calls this the *pharmacogenic defense*. Amphetamines provide an experience of exhilarating power that counteracts feelings of impotent worthlessness. Along with these dynamics, Wurmser observes, the addict establishes childlike relationships with other people, perceived as all-giving parental figures. Dick's relationship with Hackett fits the bill. Finally, prolonged drug use often represents a slow suicide, motivated by self-directed rage. Wurmser's ideas about amphetamine addiction are a close match to what we know about Dick's behavior during the worst periods of his addiction.

In fear that Dick would overdose, Hackett tried to hide his drugs, but when Dick went into withdrawal she could not bear to see him in pain. Amphetamine withdrawal is a serious medical condition and can cause anxiety, seizures, and even heart attacks. Because of the medical risks involved, clinicians usually recommend that amphetamine detox take place in a medically supervised setting, like a hospital or a drug rehabilitation facility. Even if Dick had been fully committed to abstinence from drugs, going cold turkey would have been hazardous without professional supervision. In short, Dick's physical dependence on speed had become so severe that he no longer had the ability to safely quit. Hackett gave up and handed over the pills.

By 1970, Hackett's tolerance of Dick's volatility reached its end. She had an affair with a neighbor, left Dick, and took Isolde with her. Dick was devastated. He wrote that Nancy's departure pushed him "over the brink." Moreover, for reasons that are not known, Dick's mother stopped visiting him at this time. The absence of Dick's family opened the door for his addiction to take total reign over his life. He stuffed his refrigerator with thousand-pill jars of amphetamines and protein milkshakes. He gulped handfuls of tablets and washed them down with the shakes. The idea was that at least he wouldn't be downing drugs on an empty stomach. Dick told his mother he consumed a thousand-pill jar per week. He stayed up for several nights at a time on a run, and then crashed for days. Dick had visions of menacing figures looming over his bed and lurking in the yard. In journal entries, he called the amphetamines "happiness pills" and "nightmare pills." Dick threw himself into the drug community, and his home achieved a reputation as a hangout for drug-abusing teenagers. His mind beclouded by drugs and grief for his failed marriage, Dick crossed lines that shocked his friends. To keep his underage protégés by his side, Dick provided free pills. He undertook relationships with several teenage girls, attempting to craft them into mother figures. Dick was trying, unsuccessfully, to turn back time and recreate his relationship with the young Hackett. He feared if he was alone for even a moment, he would kill himself. One girl Dick courted said he frequently asked her to marry him, and collapsed in tears when she inevitably declined.

Meanwhile, Dick's financial situation continued to hemorrhage. Speed cost $300 a month, which, adjusted for inflation, would be equivalent to about $1,700 today. Dick fell behind on his mortgage payments, and the loan company foreclosed on his house. Because Dick's mother and stepfather provided the down payment for the house, they were notified that their credit would be affected. When they talked to Dick, he promised to pay what he owed, even though he was broke. Ultimately, his parents had to pay the loan company for him. Records of Dick's phone conversations with his mother and stepfather tell a textbook story of addiction: Dick lies, demands money, and manipulates, while his parents enable.

Dick's paranoia grew. In 1971, he appeared at the door of a friend, Lynn Cecil, at 4 a.m. to complain that he had disclosed classified information in one of his books. The CIA was after him, the terrified Dick exclaimed. Dick had a session with a psychiatrist in which he declared his phone was tapped by the CIA and FBI. He even feared his mother and stepfather would steal his house. During this period, Dick hired two bodyguards to protect him from another addict whom he suspected would break into his house and murder him. Dick's house was burglarized in 1971. (In the next chapter, I explore the burglary in detail.)

After speaking at a 1972 science fiction convention in Vancouver, Canada, Dick decided to live there permanently. Because of lingering fears about the burglary, he felt safer residing outside of the United States. However, with few friends nearby, Dick was "lonely as hell . . . everyone is beginning to realize that despite my fame and my great books I am a distinct liability to know or to have anything to do with." Dick slipped into a suicidal depression and considered overdosing on drugs. Changing his mind at the last minute, he called a suicide hotline. The specific details of what happened next are unclear, but Dick ended up in a residential addiction treatment center called X-Kalay. While X-Kalay was controversial, it was the only residential addiction program available in Vancouver at the time.

X-Kalay was established in 1967 by David Berner, a charismatic figure who started the organization as a project for the Company of Young Canadians, a Canadian equivalent of the Peace Corps. X-Kalay was designed to function as a transitional community for Native Americans recently released from prison. The idea was to provide a setting in which they could be reintegrated into society. Under Berner's guidance, however, the community developed into a therapeutic program for recovering addicts. Berner, who had no formal clinical training, based his approach on a belief that addicts lacked a strong father figure. He endeavored to become the strong paternal figure he felt they needed by assuming a dictatorial role in the therapeutic community. X-Kalay offices were festooned with Berner's harsh aphorisms, such as "sympathy kills" and "My only fear is that the meek might really inherit the earth." The X-Kalay philosophy was to break new residents down, drill-sergeant fashion, by name-calling and humiliation. New residents had to clean the toilets and mop the floors. Berner's view was that any kindness shown toward the addict was a form of enabling. As part of his clinical strategy, Berner forbid residents any contact with the outside world. They were not permitted phone calls or visitors. To prevent residents from secretly using drugs, staff allowed them no privacy. They had to shower together and leave the door open while using the bathroom. Like many of the harsher addiction treatment centers, X-Kalay was a de facto cult. One government report on X-Kalay stated that the residents displayed "stereotyped responses" that indicated "massive indoctrination."

Dick's account of his three-week stay at X-Kalay suggests that although the treatment helped moderate his addiction, it was traumatic. He writes of group therapy sessions in which residents traded scathing personal accusations and gleefully attacked each other's psychological weak points. Even for the most hardened, thick-skinned ex-convict, these sessions would have been unsettling. For a man as sensitive as Dick, they were annihilating. In a letter, Dick writes that he felt like X-Kalay incinerated part of his brain. Staff prohibited any expression of emotion outside group therapy, in the belief that residents were incapable of expressing feelings without acting on them. Dick wrote that residents were being transformed into cold machines. He would later joke that perhaps the real Philip K. Dick had died in Canada, and that an android lookalike had replaced him. In his novel *A Scanner Darkly*, Dick writes of a fictional treatment program called New Path, a thinly veiled reference to X-Kalay. In Dick's novel, New Path residents endure "destruct therapy" and farm the ingredients of the very drugs to which they are addicted. In other words, X-Kalay was a hypocritical and destructive brainwash.

Although Dick reduced his drug use after leaving X-Kalay, his paranoia remained. Quitting speed does not necessarily free the addict from amphetamine psychosis. Paranoia and other symptoms often remain, and can take years to fade away. Sometimes, they are permanent. Dick moved to Fullerton, California, but refused to disclose the new address to acquaintances. Tim Powers, a young writer who befriended Dick at the time, recalls that he was vigilant to small anomalies in his environment and read them as signs of encroaching malevolent forces. He became alarmed when he noticed large numbers of radios in cars parked near his home or heard the engines of cars in the night. Throughout the early 1970s, he continued to ruminate about the burglary of his home, sending letters to the FBI and to the county sheriff claiming he was being persecuted by a neo-Nazi conspiracy because of cryptic messages buried in his novels.

In 1972, Dick married the 18-year-old Tessa Busby, an aspiring writer he met at a party. She writes in her memoir *My Life on the Edge of Reality* that when she first met Dick, he thought she was a spy. Even after he got comfortable with her, he was hard to live with. She paints a picture of a regressed and explosive man who often needed to be rocked and held like a baby. Sometimes, Dick subjected her to the "attack therapy" he had endured at X-Kalay, exploiting her psychological vulnerabilities. When Dick was angry, he stamped his feet and ripped his shirt open like the Incredible Hulk. Dick writes that he often called Tessa "Dummy" and seems perplexed that she took umbrage at this pet name. Tessa gave birth to a son, Christopher, in 1973. Philip reacted with what he referred to as a postpartum depression, felt suicidal again, and was psychiatrically hospitalized for three weeks.

The Exploding Self

The theme of self-destruction through self-discovery runs through these years of Dick's life like a red thread. Whether it was through abuse of mind-altering drugs, relationships that reenacted his traumatic past, or outright suicide attempts, Dick searched for himself in the abyss. Because of the die messages he received as a child, he was trapped in a vicious circle. Insofar as his mother held him responsible for his twin's death, he felt he was born of destructiveness, and *because* he felt that way, he had to *be* destructive to be true to himself. By 1974 Dick had destroyed several marriages, broken countless friendships, and ruined his body with drugs. Dick was Spence Olham, Rachel Rosen, and Garson Poole wrapped up into one. Like these android characters, he could not escape his origins. In Dick's reality tape, the same traumatic experiences replayed again and again, and they always ended in devastation.

That said, underlying Dick's destructiveness was not only rage, but also hope. Like Garson Poole, Dick hoped that annihilation of the self might lead to transformation. In a paper entitled "Masochism, Submission, and Surrender," famous in psychotherapy circles, the psychoanalyst Emmanuel Ghent proposes that self-destructiveness is linked to a basic human longing for recognition and growth, which requires one to let go of psychological masks so that the true self can emerge and be known. Ghent calls this process *surrender*. Surrender, for Ghent, means a relaxing of defenses, a letting-go of resistances, in the service of growth. Ghent warns that the longing for surrender can be defensively warped into a desire for self-harm, leading to self-destructive acting out: a "perversion of surrender." From Ghent's standpoint, then, what Dick was after was self-transformation through surrender. However, the need for surrender was perverted into self-annihilation through addiction, explosiveness, and suicidality. Dick meant to kill off a false self in order to uncover who he truly was. He was trying to tear through his own mask. In a way, his quest for self-destruction was a quest for truth.

6 | COUNTERFEIT BURGLARY

On November 17, 1971, Dick's paranoid fears were realized. He came home to find that his house appeared to have been burglarized. His massive stereo system was missing, windows were smashed, the locks on his doors were destroyed, and his specially reinforced file cabinet was broken open. The floor was wet and covered in asbestos.

At the time, Dick lived in a gritty neighborhood in San Rafael, California. In the wake of his separation from Nancy Hackett, he had opened his home to a motley cast of young drifters and drug dealers. Devastated by the break with Nancy, Dick found the presence of the young delinquents comforting. He said he needed the constant companionship to stop him from killing himself. It may also be that because he had regressed while being mothered by Hackett, he felt most comfortable relating to the young. Local teenagers knew that if they needed a place to sleep or eat, Philip Dick's house was available. Some were addicts who either received amphetamines from Dick or shared a drug dealer with him. Like Dick, "Rick" and "Daniel" were addicts in the grip of paranoia. Daniel, a musician in his twenties, had hallucinations that insects were crawling all over his body. He sprayed himself with Raid to fight off the insect engulfment, a strategy sometimes resulting in hospitalization. Rick tormented Daniel by pretending to throw bugs at him. Rick, who believed he was under surveillance by the FBI, stored fifteen rifles under his bed. Although Dick agreed the FBI was watching, he wisely appropriated Rick's ammunition and removed the firing pins from his guns. Dick suspected Rick was plotting his murder and kicked him out of the house in early 1971. Both these men were immortalized as characters in Dick's *A Scanner Darkly*. For Dick, the two seem to have personified aspects of his own addiction.

"Cindy," a teenage friend who was the inspiration for characters in three of Dick's novels, was a high school delinquent who worked at a nearby fish and chips joint. She was also the girlfriend of Dick's drug dealer, a Hell's Angels biker. Part of Cindy's appeal was her dark hair and eyes, features that made her an irresistible target for Dick's obsession with dark-haired girls who resembled what his twin sister might have looked like had she lived. Dick wrote that for him, Cindy represented youth. He said Cindy was a thief who once stole several cases of Coca-Cola from a delivery truck so she could turn in the empty bottles for cash. She had a conflictual relationship with her parents, and came to Dick for sympathy. When she became pregnant in her junior year of high school, Dick helped set up an abortion. To some extent, the caretaking was mutual: Dick wrote a letter thanking Cindy for her "wise and dispassionate guidance."

Cindy recalls that once, Dick hid his stash of speed underneath some plants in the yard, and forgot where it was. Later, he dug up half of the yard before finding the drugs. She characterized Dick's house as a "sort of paradise" for the young, filled with "lots of pot, free drugs, beer, wine, imported Player cigarettes, aqua filters, and little cans of different flavored snuff all around the house." Dick suspected

Cindy of conspiring to rob him. However, he was so enamored of her that he protected her from future prosecution by preparing a document granting her the right to use anything he owned.

Another teenager, "Sheila," was a runaway who lived at Dick's house. She describes Dick as paranoid and incoherent. As Sheila puts it, "He used to do a handful [of speed] at a time, several times a day, for a week or two, and then he'd sleep for two or three days. I used to wonder why he was getting crazy, and then I caught on that after a few days on a binge, he'd get real crazy, then he'd need to sleep, and then he'd be okay for awhile again." Dick hid his Hugo Award—which he earned for *The Man in the High Castle*—in fear that his housemates would steal it. Sheila says that after an argument with his ex-wife Nancy, Dick was frightened that her boyfriend would try to kill him. He hired three men with shotguns to guard him for three days until the danger passed. Often, she noted, Dick treated everyone in the house to food and clothing. Once again, he attempted to play the role of savior. But rescuing carried the danger of victimization, for his kindness could be taken for weakness. He gave too much, and was fearful that more would be asked of him. Dick became obsessed with Sheila and proposed marriage. She declined. His marriage to the young Nancy had recently ended, and perhaps he hoped to make up for the loss by marrying another young woman. When she tried to flee the house, Dick detained her by seizing her clothes. Sheila redoubled her efforts to remove herself from his orbit when mysterious thefts and damages began to occur. Someone stole all the doorknobs in the house, and the wires to Dick's amplifier were cut. Sheila finally made her escape by entering an inpatient drug rehabilitation program.

Not only were Dick's interactions with his housemates volatile, but he also had a fraught relationship with the police. Because of Dick's paranoia, he often called the police and said he was about to be killed or robbed. The police chastised him for calling too much. Dick saw a frightening shadow behind his house late at night, and received menacing anonymous phone calls. The police told him to buy a gun to protect himself. Dick complained that the CIA and FBI were sneaking into his house and stealing his papers. As I mentioned earlier, the belief that one's personal belongings are being secretly stolen is a typical persecutory delusion, and might be chalked up to Dick's amphetamine psychosis, which was in high gear. The trouble is, the November break-in seemed to confirm these beliefs. It was as if reality had shaped itself to match Dick's paranoid fears.

As Dick tells the story, on the night of the burglary he went out to buy dinner. After he drove a few blocks, black smoke billowed from his engine. Terrified that his car had been sabotaged and he was in imminent danger, Dick raced away. He called a tow truck, and after several hours, the car was towed. When he returned to his house, he found it a wreck. Dick had anticipated a break-in, and had nailed the windows shut and placed locks on the doors. Marks on several doors and windows made it appear that burglars had tried to enter there but failed, and managed to gain access by breaking through a window. In Dick's version of the story, the burglars drilled two holes in the file cabinet and pushed plastic explosives into them. Dick theorized that the floor was wet because the burglars used wet towels to contain the explosion. Although I emphasize Dick's narrative of these events, there is a genuine police report and witnesses to the destruction. The damage was real. That said, the police report indicates that the file cabinet was drilled or pried open, *not* blown apart. Also, Dick's housemate Daniel had irreparably destroyed the locks of the file cabinet a month or two earlier. The cabinet, in other words, was unlocked.

As for what was in the files, they mostly contained Dick's papers, including business documents and notes for potential stories and novels. However, Dick says he also kept a gun in the cabinet, which disappeared. Oddly, Dick's jewelry collection was not stolen, even though it too was in the file cabinets. Nor was any money stolen. According to Dick, one item taken in excess was checkbooks: "they'd taken a sample checkbook of every checking account they could find, of new checks, unused checks." When the police arrived, they told Dick to make a list of the missing items and bring it to the police station. Dick stayed overnight at the home of another sci-fi writer, Avram Davidson. The next day Dick went to the precinct to hand in the list, but was told there had been no robbery the night before. He was informed that no police had come to his home. Two police officers were then sent to the house to investigate, and promptly accused Dick of burglarizing his own house for insurance reimbursement. However, Dick had no insurance. Ultimately, the officers decided there had indeed been a burglary, but they could identify no suspects. Soon after, Dick fled to Vancouver, Canada, where he stayed until March of the following year undergoing inpatient drug rehabilitation treatment at X-Kalay.

Dick was fascinated by the conundrum that the break-in presented. It became a sort of fixed idea of the kind common in speed addiction. According to his friend Avram Davidson, during the night of the break-in Dick was "baffled" yet also "intrinsically undisturbed, marveling at the efficiency of the job." Who had perpetrated it and why? Why were the checkbooks taken and not the jewelry? The 1971 break-in inspired him to creatively theorize about it for years, and was the subject of a famous *Rolling Stone* article by Paul Williams.

Dick's theories of the break-in ranged from the disturbing to the outrageous. One of the most commonsense notions was that the burglary was perpetrated by one or more of the many criminals who hung around Dick's house. Loren Cavit, Dick's friend, supposed the perpetrator must have been someone close enough to Dick to know when he was not home, because he usually was in the house. After all, someone in the house had already stolen the doorknobs, so what would stop the same person from pulling off a more substantial heist? Also, there was tension between Dick and his young housemates, and it would be unsurprising if they had chosen to rob him as retribution for his maddening behavior. Dick was already frightened that the rifle-toting Rick planned to assassinate him. Alternatively, perhaps one of the many addicts frequenting Dick's home needed to make some quick cash. Ray Nelson, another friend of Dick's, claims he kept a bag of heroin in his file cabinet and that perhaps some of the younger addicts stole it. The list of suspects named by this theory is long: after all, Dick's home was an open house for Marin County drug users, and addiction and theft go hand in hand.

A more dubious theory Dick cooked up was that his home was raided by religious zealots seeking to dig up dirt on the heretical doctrines of the Bishop James Pike, Dick's deceased friend. The basis for the Pike theory was that the stolen files included, among many other things, information on Pike. Dick wondered if the burglars believed the stolen files might be helpful in discrediting Pike. There is little logical sense to be made of the Pike theory, as it is not clear what anyone would gain by further besmirching Pike's reputation, nor who would go to such lengths to do so. Perhaps the Pike theory is best seen as a gesture of protectiveness towards Dick's departed friend.

Dick also concocted a theory that the break-in was perpetrated by military intelligence or the CIA. The CIA theory has it that Dick inadvertently revealed military secrets in his science fiction novels. The obvious question would be: how would he have gained access to such secrets in the first place? After all, the closest Dick had ever come to the military was a brief college fling with the ROTC. A friend, Lynn Cecil, said that Dick claimed to have "written something in one of his books that corresponded with something true and the CIA was interested." Startlingly, Dick was not entirely wrong about being under CIA surveillance. In 1958, he wrote to a Soviet physicist about research discrediting Einstein, and his letter was seized by the CIA. More importantly, in 1968 Dick signed a famous petition for the radical magazine *Ramparts* that asked U.S. citizens to withhold taxes in protest of the Vietnam War. He feared government retaliation for the petition. Fears of government intrusions were in the air at that time, the era of Watergate. Nevertheless, it seems unlikely the CIA would risk engaging in a burglary operation in retaliation for a signature on a petition, nor in order to explore a tenuous linkage between a science fiction novel and possible espionage activity.

Another incredible theory Dick took quite seriously was that he was attacked by a neo-Nazi group. In the letter he sent to the

FBI in October 1972, Dick claims he was contacted by one such outfit intent on recruiting science fiction writers. Dick says the agent identified himself as "Solarcon-6." He claims Solarcon-6 instructed him to embed coded messages in his novels to be deciphered by neo-Nazi readers. Dick writes, "I was approached by an individual who I have reason to believe belonged to a covert organization involved in politics, illegal weapons, etc., who put great pressure on me to place coded information in future novels 'to be read by the right people here and there', as he phrased it. I refused to do this." According to Dick, the neo-Nazis hoped to spark World War III through germ warfare, planning to introduce a lethal strain of syphilis into the U.S. population. He believed another science fiction writer, Thomas Disch, was recruited by Solarcon and had hidden neo-Nazi messages in his novel *Camp Concentration*.

In a second letter on the same topic, this one written to the police, Dick proposes that Solarcon was behind the 1972 break-in. He identifies Solarcon-6 as his friend Harold Kinchen: "Beyond any doubt, Kinchen is an ardent Nazi trained in such skills as weapons-use, explosives, wire-tapping, chemistry, psychology, toxins and poisons, electronics, auto repair, sabotage, the manufacture of narcotics. . . . What I did not pass on to anyone, because I feared for my life, is the fact that Kinchen put coercive pressure, both physical and psychological, on me to put secret coded information into my future published writings." The FBI and police discounted Dick's letters, however, as he provided no evidence for his accusations. His letters were ignored. The FBI concluded, "The information reflected in those letters was presumption only on [Dick's] part regarding neo-nazism and Minutemen. He did not have any further business or substantiation, names of individuals, or additional information to which he had previously furnished."

A fourth theory of Dick's was that the break-in was racially motivated. His neighborhood was predominantly African-American, and 1972 was a time of racial tension. Dick claimed that a number of Caucasians who lived in the area were forced out by militant African-American groups. Dick said he had encounters with individuals he described as Black Panthers. Once he hired several African-American men he claimed were Black Panthers to guard him. They asked him for several hundred dollars immediately. He gave it to them, and they left without doing any guarding. It was a rip-off. It is clear Dick's perception of race, like his perception of nearly everything, was shaped by his paranoia: although he claims to have African-American friends, he portrays his African-American neighbors as objects of dread.

Dick also wondered if the police broke into his house to investigate drug activity. This theory, too, had a slight basis in reality. The local police apparently perceived Dick as a Timothy Leary–like figure who was a charismatic drug guru to local teenagers. Maybe the police illegally broke into Dick's home searching for drugs, and tried to cover their tracks by making the break-in look like a burglary. After the break-in, a policeman supposedly asked Dick if he planned to "start up operations again." If that were the case, it might explain why the police later told Dick that there had been no burglary. Let's call this explanation of the break-in the Bungled Police Operation Theory. In light of Dick's contact with the police and the drug activity in his home, the Bungled Police Operation Theory isn't completely implausible. He had the attention of the local authorities, and their attention was not benign.

In a 1972 journal entry, Dick writes "A police sergeant in Marin County warned me that if I didn't leave 'I'd probably get a bullet in my back some night or worse.' He further said, 'This county doesn't need a crusader,' referring to me."

Finally, there was the theory with which the police confronted Dick: that he perpetrated the break-in himself. Far from rejecting it, Dick was intrigued by this idea. Although he had no insurance, he was saddled with a large tax debt. Dick might have intended to evade the IRS by making his financial records disappear. He offered more dramatic explanations, conjecturing that he destroyed his own file cabinet because he was programmed to do so by posthypnotic suggestion, or because he was psychotic. Although posthypnotic suggestions only produce such dramatic results in the movies, it is possible that Dick attacked his own home in a psychotic fit. After all, there are no witnesses to verify that Dick was absent from his house when it was burglarized. Maybe the broken-down car story was fabricated as an alibi. Or, perhaps his car did break down, triggering a paranoid episode that drove Dick to fake a burglary of his own house. It would be a characteristically Philip K. Dickian move for him to burglarize his own home because of fear of surveillance. He would have beaten the enemy to the punch, so to speak. I'll call this theory the Doppelganger Theory, aligning it with the Deadly Double theme of Dick's life. Although several commentators have treated the Doppelganger Theory as an amusing fiction and nothing more, there is more substance to it than that.

Let's explore how Dick might have proceeded to fake the burglary of his own home. Under increasing pressure from the

IRS, and afraid that his files contained coveted information, he may have decided that his circumstances were untenable. He could escape neither the IRS nor the CIA, and time was ticking. Desperately seeking a way out, Dick might have hoped to side-step the encroaching government agencies by throwing them off the scent with a fake burglary. The IRS would have no checks to examine, and the CIA would have no files to spy on. It could be, then, that when he noticed that the family living in the house behind him was away, he seized the opportunity to fake a burglary without being detected. Dick systematically broke his own windows and smashed his own locks. Then, he pried his own file cabinet open. He removed his files and, for good measure, his expensive stereo system to demonstrate that it was a genuine burglary (for what burglar would pass up an expensive stereo system?). However, he left his jewelry in the cabinet because it had sentimental value. Throwing everything in his car, Dick drove far away and dumped it. Next, he either sabotaged his own car, or simply lied when he later claimed to have had it towed. Dick did not call the police that night, and that was why there was no report of a burglary. Instead, he penned a list of the items he dumped and brought it to the precinct the next day. When the police inspectors arrived, they quite rightly smelled a con act and accused Dick of breaking into his own house. Yet since Dick lacked insurance, they could not convincingly argue motive, so they chose to blame the burglary on unknown perpetrators in order to close the case.

Although the Doppelganger Theory is bizarre, it is consistent with what we know of Dick's psychological functioning at the time of the break-in, which was rife with irrational behavior, paranoia, and episodes of dissociative amnesia. Dick often did odd and destructive things and forgot them. According to the Doppelganger Theory, the inconsistencies in the crime scene were the inconsistencies of Dick's own personality, stamped in wet asbestos. The Doppelganger Theory is the only theory that accounts for everything. It explains why the police found no identifiable footprints, why there were no suspects, why Dick was calm about the burglary the night it happened, why he would say that doorknobs that had already gone missing were smashed, and why unlocked file cabinets would need to be pried open. Dick was his own burglar, his own persecutor, his own deadly double.

There is one snag with the Doppelganger Theory: Although Dick conjectures he might have been responsible for the break-in, he never openly *admits* it even in his private journals. The Doppelganger Theory, then, would have to posit that not only did Dick burglarize his own home, but that he later forgot having done it. However, amnesia is not as preposterous an explanation as it may seem. Dick routinely had dissociated moments that he later forgot. In an interview with Paul Williams, he and his fifth wife Tessa verify the extent of the amnesia:

> "It'd be like, an example would be, suppose tomorrow you [Paul Williams] fly away from here, and if this was all a traumatic experience, or if there was a lot of anxiety in it for me, would be that next week I would say to Tess, 'Gee, I wonder when Paul Williams is gonna come and interview me,' see? And then she'd say, 'He just did, last week!' And I'd say, 'I don't remember that at all'."

From the perspective of Dick's conscious mind, then, he left his house to buy some dinner, then things got hazy, and a few hours later he was standing in his study in a pile of rubble without remembering what happened. The amnesia worked perfectly. That way, Dick could make a police report without lying. His amnesia gave him honesty.

Not only that, but by burglarizing his own home, Dick provided proof validating his paranoid fears. People who have persecutory delusions are repeatedly confronted with others' skepticism. When they communicate their delusions to other people, they are met with doubt. Over time, that doubt can feel invalidating, contributing to desperate efforts to prove the reality of the delusions. Paranoid people have been known to forge documents, provoke violence, and even mutilate themselves to show they are victims of persecution. Consistent with this feature of paranoia, Dick's narrations of the burglary to interviewers show a tendency to reach excessively for validation. During interviews, Dick frequently calls upon imaginary witnesses and experts, such as explosives experts whom he supposedly consulted, lawyers who allegedly said he was a victim of religious persecution, and a phantom cab driver who supposedly witnessed the crime scene but was never to be found. Dick invents authorities to buttress his claims because they are not credible. In a 1977 interview at a science fiction convention, for example, Dick assures his audience that "my attorneys said it [the burglary] was the government, that there was no doubt that it was the government." By putting his own paranoia into the mouths of others, Dick enhanced his own credibility.

Numerous similar moments appear in rock journalist Paul Williams' 1974 interviews of Dick, originally done for the *Rolling*

Stone article on the break-in. The Williams interview was inspired by a letter Dick sent to Williams in November 1972. In the letter, Dick writes:

"Somebody just about got me back about a year ago; I came home and found my files blown open with plastic military explosives, windows smashed in, doorlocks smashed, everything of value gone such as stereo, business records and cancelled checks, correspondence and papers gone, rubble everywhere. . . . I got threatening phone calls saying the next time it'd be worse . . . one arrest, much later, of a Panther, with my gun stolen from my files that night . . . In the wet rubble on the floors: big combat boot footprints . . . I was shucked by deadly people playing a deadly game: I saw a lot of guns, explosives, silencers—they used blackmail on me, terror and psychological intimidation . . . They even tried to involve me in murder, conspiracy to commit murder, saying it was the only way I could save my own life."

Again, it is not evident that explosives were used: that's Dick's embellishment. When Dick says "everything of value was gone," he makes a false statement. After all, the jewelry wasn't taken. His remark about the footprints is also inconsistent with his other accounts. Elsewhere, Dick claims he found a single partial boot print in asbestos that somehow got in his closet, and that the boot print was missed by the police because they did not look there. Even if we choose to believe the story of the unseen closet boot print, Dick vacillates between claiming he saw a single print and plural prints. The inconsistency of his claim casts doubt on its veracity. Then Dick refers to having "seen" guns and explosives and silencers—where? If he had seen these, why does he not describe them elsewhere? At best, Dick's letter to Williams gives a fictionalized version of the break-in, and as I'll show, it has major discrepancies with his later accounts.

As the interview begins, Williams asks Dick to tell him about the break-in. Dick replies that he often rehearsed his story, and "shaped it into an absolutely authentic record of what happened." A remark like this might seem innocuous on the surface, but it raises doubts. Why did Dick need to "shape" his narrative of the break-in into an "absolutely authentic record"? Why wasn't it absolutely authentic to start with? And why emphasize the authenticity of the narrative at all? By stressing the absolute authenticity of his story, does Dick protest too much? Finally, aren't "shaping" and authenticity oxymoronic?

A few moments later in the interview, Dick describes the crime scene: "my house was in ruins, my files were blown up, my papers were gone, my stereo was gone, the windows were smashed in, the doorknobs were smashed off, the hasps were pulled off—with rubble all over the floor." As I mentioned above, both the police report and witnesses to the scene state that the files were "pried open," not "blown up." An even more striking discrepancy is Dick's claim that the doorknobs were smashed off when in fact his doorknobs had already gone missing prior to the break-in. Did Dick forget that his doorknobs had already disappeared? Or did he lie about the doorknobs, and if so, why?

Dick elaborates: "they had smashed in one window—and in coming in and finding doors shut, they had smashed the knobs and locks right off the doors. The noise must have been quite severe at that point, doing that, must have been quite loud." Dick repeats the falsehood about the doorknobs, and adds a tangential remark about the noise. Why was the noise of interest? Did Dick wonder if anyone overheard the burglary? Or was he experiencing hints of a dim, dissociated memory fragment of how loud it was when he *himself* smashed the locks?

Then, Dick says he asked the cabdriver who drove him home to look at the scene: "I turned and got the cab, ran back and got the cabdriver to come and look at it, and—we'd talked on the way, he was a real tough dude, he was a biker—he took one look at it and said, 'I won't go in that house'." Dick says he took the cabbie's number and asked him to speak to the police, but he drove off. The "tough dude" description seems to be a means of validating Dick's fears. Dick is saying, in essence, that the situation was so scary even a "tough dude" was afraid of it. If so, Dick implies, his own fears were valid. Two features of the cabdriver narrative are suspect. For one thing, why didn't the cabdriver drive off immediately after dropping Dick off? How was Dick able to run back and get him? Also, even if the cabdriver drove off after seeing the house, why didn't Dick call him later and have him speak to the police on the phone? Given these discrepancies, it is safe to assume that the cabdriver either dropped Dick off without witnessing the crime scene, or was a figment of Dick's imagination. He was either irrelevant or a phantom.

Next, Dick talks about the water on the floor. He says "the water was from towels that had been soaked in water; they were all heaped up in the bathroom shower and it was easy to see that they had been put over the file when it was blown." Dick does not answer the obvious question: if these soaked towels were placed over the file cabinet when it was blown, then why were they so thoughtfully piled up in the bathroom shower rather than destroyed and lying all over the floor, like the asbestos? One answer: because Dick piled them up in the shower himself.

Next, Dick tries to support his claim that his files were blown open by plastic explosives, a conjecture with which *no one else who saw the crime scene agrees.* He appeals to the expertise of a Special Forces soldier he claims he met in the hospital while undergoing surgery for a shoulder injury in 1972. He provides no name, and there is no one who could verify that the hospital conversation occurred. The soldier, Dick says, told him that wet towels were necessary to contain the explosion, and that if they were not used the entire room would have been filled with a "sheet of flame," the windows blown out. Dick says the soldier was somehow able to determine the type of explosive used, and claimed it was a "C3 or C4," which he said makes "no sound." In fact, both types of plastic explosive make significant noise. Did the soldier actually exist? Even if the conversation truly occurred, how would Dick have known if the soldier was on the level? These questions are unanswered.

Dick next turns to the stolen checks. The burglars "had taken every check in the house, going back over twenty years. They had gotten every single one. That had taken quite a bit of time. And they knew just where to look. And, uh, I have no theory about why they did that." The Doppelganger Theory would have it that in a dissociated state of mind, Dick grabbed all his own cancelled checks and destroyed them to reduce his anxiety about the IRS. He knew where to look because he knew where he had put them.

The absence of the cancelled checks is one of the most telling aspects of the crime scene. There is no one other than Dick who could have known where all of his cancelled checks were located.

Dick then tells Williams his lawyer saw the damage too and it was "the kind of thing that military training—that he had had in the service, and they were taught to do it." However, it seems unlikely military training would teach one how to burglarize an apartment, let alone blow open file cabinets. It appears Dick is trying to transform his lawyer into another Special Forces demolition expert, a second version of the soldier from the hospital, to authenticate his plastic explosives theory. Several interpretations come to mind. Perhaps Dick's lawyer saw the damage and Dick himself argued that it was military, and in order to placate Dick, his lawyer agreed. Alternatively, perhaps there was no such discussion at all. Whatever Dick's attorney actually said, it is unlikely that the average attorney would have the expertise to analyze a crime scene. It is as if Dick hopes that by increasing the number of his dubious sources, he will increase their credibility.

Dick complains to Williams about one of the police officers' reaction to the crime scene. "After looking around he smiled and asked me why I'd done it . . . He looked around and he says . . . 'what I wonder is why did you scatter all the asbestos all around, why did you do *that*?' And laughed." The voice of reality intrudes on Dick's narrative. After citing so many spurious authorities—the phantom cabdriver, the unknown hospital soldier, the attorney with military training—he finally mentions *credible* authorities: the police officers who analyzed the crime scene. They immediately perceive the burglary to be Dick's own doing, and do so with confidence. Dick says he replied to the police defensively, exclaiming, "You guys are really crazy. You got no record of a robbery, you tell me that I did it, my house is a shambles, I can't live in it. Look at this file's been blown up." Notice the move Dick makes here. He tries to convince the police that they, not he, are acting "crazy." Several of Dick's friends note that he often behaved irrationally and then tried to convince the other person that he or she was "crazy." To attempt to persuade the police that *they* were crazy in order to nullify their perception of *him* as crazy would be a typical maneuver on his part. In the Williams interview, the "crazy" police represent the voice of reality Dick must ward off to prevent himself from remembering he had destroyed his own home. In dismissing the police, Dick also dismisses the part of himself that dimly recognizes the truth in their accusation.

Next, Dick marshals the evidence in favor of his theory that his house was burgled by black militants. He claims that members of an African-American family living in a house behind his were terrorists. However, he does not provide names. Dick declares that he received information on these individuals' criminal histories by the police, who showed pictures. However, he contradicts himself, saying he was not able to identify the individuals in the pictures the police showed him, nor did he recognize their names. Finally, and confusingly, he says the people in the police pictures were prisoners residing in San Quentin, so apparently not living in the house behind him at all! During the night of the burglary and for several weeks later, Dick says, the family's house was empty. He implies that their absence is cause for suspicion.

There is no proof any of these claims are false, but all of them are dubious. Dick is known to have falsely accused his neighbor

Honor Jackson of being a Black Panther after Jackson had an affair with Dick's wife. The racial tint of Dick's logic makes it look as if he believed that being African-American was itself, somehow, a cause for suspicion. To be black, for Dick, was to be at risk of being a Panther. Dick might defend himself by exclaiming, as he does in the interview, that he had many African-American friends. Nevertheless, the Black Panther theory is based largely on racial profiling. Take away the racial profiling, and all that is left is a vague suspicion of nameless convicts lurking in the neighborhood. The Black Panther theory is racial paranoia, pure and simple.

Consistent with my reading, Dick says that a gun he alleges was stolen from his house was later found in the possession of an African-American man. The man, he says, was arrested by a "separate police agency." What Dick means by that is unclear. At any rate, the alleged arrest of the man with the alleged gun by the unknown police agency somehow, for Dick, becomes proof that the Black Panthers were involved in the burglary. Dick goes on to claim that he saw the man with the gun speaking to the family who lived behind him. It is as if he initially believes that skin color is sufficient grounds to link burglar to family and to terrorist, and then, in midstream, realizes that a stronger link is needed. Dick tries to fashion that link by alleging that he saw the man with the gun speaking to the family. Finally, he assures his interviewer that everything he saw "synchronize[d] with police information." Yet that remark conflicts with his earlier assertion that the police had said men *in* the family behind his house were criminals, not a man who *talked to* the family. So, the police information Dick initially cites does not actually "synchronize" with his later claims, although it does not directly contradict them. Whatever the facts of the matter truly are, whatever Dick did or did not see, his reasoning is tendentious. The identity of the individual he wishes to indict shifts back and forth between his neighbors, to a man he saw speaking to them, to nonspecific "black militants" he says dominated the neighborhood. Who is Dick accusing of what, exactly?

As the interview proceeds, Dick piles on more spurious justifications for the Black Panther Theory. He later says a "very astute person" suggested aspects of the theory even though it had "never occurred to me." It is the same pattern as before: Dick invents an authority and places his own suspicions in that authority's mouth. That way, Dick doesn't have to accept responsibility for his own conjectures. He portrays his conspiracy theories as the sober hypotheses of venerable experts. It is important to emphasize that although Dick implies that the Black Panther Theory was offered by others, it is in fact his own theory. The other people to whom he refers are there to buttress his own illogical justifications.

Eventually, Dick flips the theory, suggesting the perpetrators of the break-in were government agents investigating Dick's *own* involvement with "black militants." As evidence for this theory, Dick notes that after he abandoned his house and moved to Vancouver "all the remaining business papers disappeared." Sounds suspicious, indeed! But then Dick clarifies: "All of them. From both desks. The contents of both desks . . . And the desks. Disappeared." It wasn't that the business papers disappeared per se, as Dick initially said. As he elaborates, it becomes clear that his desks were taken, and with them, naturally, the papers inside them. In fact, that version of the story seems to work against Dick's government conspiracy theory. For why would government agents need the desks? Why not just take the papers, as Dick initially implied? The evidence that Dick offers turns out to be worse than no evidence at all. Rather than supporting the government conspiracy theory, it gainsays it.

Returning to the missing checks, Dick next speculates that there were counterfeit checks going through his bank account. His interviewer challenges him, noting that Dick could investigate whether forged checks were used. Dick protests that he asked his bank for photocopies of the checks, but his bank did not comply and his bank officer was suspiciously transferred. Dick's theory seems to require that the bank itself was involved in the conspiracy, a hard-to-swallow proposition that casts doubt on the theory. It is hard to believe that a bank would collude with forgery, although a bank trafficking in counterfeit checks might make for a good Philip K. Dick story.

Dick draws a parallel between the burglary and the infamous covert investigation squad known as the Plumbers, a Nixon administration unit tasked with preventing government leaks. In September 1971 the Plumbers broke into the files of Daniel Fielding, a psychiatrist treating an antiwar activist, Daniel Ellsberg. The Plumbers hoped to find information to use against Ellsberg, who was responsible for a major leak of classified information. Dick claims he saw a TV program showing that the Fielding file cabinet was "blown in very much the same manner" as his. In fact, though, the Fielding cabinet was not blown open at all, but pried. Even the most cursory glance at the Fielding file cabinet, which remains on display at the National Museum of American History, reveals that the cabinet was obviously pried open. If Dick means to say that the damage to his file cabinet was similar to that of the

Fielding file cabinet, he yet again undermines his claim that plastic explosives were used. There is nothing at all about the Fielding break-in that suggests explosives were involved.

Further elaborating on the government conspiracy theory, Dick cites a famous case of government intrusion into science fiction that happened during World War II. In 1944, a short sci-fi story by Steve Cartmill entitled "Deadline" was targeted for FBI investigation. In writing "Deadline," Cartmill used scientific articles on nuclear bombs as source material for a story about the construction of a powerful bomb. Military scientists who were actually constructing a nuclear bomb detected uncanny similarities between Cartmill's story and their own work, and the FBI was enlisted to investigate. Although no one was charged, Cartmill's editor, John W. Campbell, was asked to delay the publication of any similar stories until after the war was over. Dick wonders if similarly, without realizing it, he had written a story whose contents were too close a match to classified projects. He speculates that the government ransacked his files to determine if he had classified documents. The novel Dick identifies as the possible culprit is *The Penultimate Truth*, in which two governments agree to sustain a war in order to keep their citizens subdued. Perhaps, Dick says, the story was too close to the truth for comfort, and government operatives acted to prevent future "leaks." Still, Dick offers no evidence in support of the government conspiracy theory. It is pure fantasy.

In a later interview, Dick narrates the events leading up to the break-in. He asserts that "Early that morning I was sure the house was going to be hit that night." Dick provides no reason why he felt sure the house would be "hit" and also fails to explain why he let it happen if he knew it was coming. What seems most psychologically likely is Dick had an impulse to hit his own house that night, which he projected onto imaginary persecutors. Consistent with my reading, Dick says when he entered his house and saw the wreckage, his reaction was "Thank God! You know why? Because, I had been saying, like Barbara had been saying before me, I had been saying to the police, and to my friends, and to myself, 'I know I have enemies, I know they are going to hit this house . . .'" Dick's immediate response was not fear, but *relief.* He felt better. He no longer needed to worry about his imaginary enemies, since "they" already struck. Even better, because his financial documents vanished, he would not have to worry about providing them to the IRS. The counterfeit break-in treated his anxiety. It was a dramatic form of self-medication. If the break-in had not happened, Dick tells his interviewer, "otherwise I would've been nuts, because she [his girlfriend] and I were in a state of absolute, abject terror. Standing there with a loaded gun, hour after hour in the dark, waiting for those people to burst in, and our friends saying 'They're nuts. They're crazy . . .' It was a *relief* to see this. Because it proved that I wasn't nuts."

7 | THE PINK LIGHT

B efore the alien pink light started blasting him in February of 1974, Dick was in trouble. The course of attack therapy at X-Kalay and the psychiatric hospitalization of 1973 had taken their toll, leaving Dick shaken. The IRS, who seized his car in 1971, continued to hound him for back taxes. Dick was afraid they would seize his assets again. Also, his relationship with Tessa, his fifth wife, was turbulent. Dick was afraid that Tessa might suddenly abandon him, and on bad days he became enraged if she left him alone for more than a half-hour. Dick's phobias and paranoid fears had become so paralyzing that he was rarely able to leave the house. There is a vicious cycle that can develop in anxious people. People often respond to anxiety with avoidance, withdrawing from what makes them nervous. Ironically, however, lack of contact with what they fear makes the feared object loom larger in their imaginations. In the long run, avoidance leads to greater anxiety, which in turn leads to greater avoidance. By February of 1974, Dick was so incapacitated by the vicious cycle of his anxieties that he could not bring himself to go to the bank to deposit his royalty checks, and had to rely on Tessa to do so.

To be sure, some of Dick's fears had a basis in reality. He had paid no taxes in years and it was natural to expect the IRS to take action against him. Also, he was nearly broke and Tessa had just given birth to a baby boy. Dick was overwhelmed and backed into a corner. In a 1978 journal entry, he writes: "I suffered total psychosis in 1974. Poverty, family responsibility (a new baby) did it. & fear of the IRS." On top of everything else, Dick was in pain from an impacted tooth. He had it extracted, but the surgery was botched and he was left in more pain than before. His physician prescribed Percodan, a pain-relieving opiate-based medication. Dick was already on a diuretic medication for high blood pressure. He also saw a psychiatrist regularly for psychotropic medications, which according to some sources included lithium, a drug used to treat mood swings. Some assert that he was still abusing amphetamines. If indeed that was the case, it must have been covert, as Tessa did not observe Dick using speed. Then again, Dick had hidden his drug use from his wife Anne, too. Whatever his precise medication regimen, it is clear he was stuffed full of all sorts of drugs that may have had a variety of physical and mental side effects. There were many elements, then, that set the stage for his bout of divine madness in 1974.

In what follows, I try to describe as rigorously as possible the actual experiences Dick had during 2-3-74. For now, I focus on description rather than explanation: more on *what* Dick experienced, rather than *why*. From my perspective, to understand the *why* one first has to nail down the *what*. To figure out what Dick's divine madness meant, we first need to know of what exactly it consisted. The existing versions of 2-3-74 leave out important details and fail to address significant discrepancies. In the narrative below, I stitch together several accounts of 2-3-74 –including those provided by Dick and his wife Tessa, who was with him throughout most of the experience- to establish the most plausible version of events.

Fish Sign Activation

Dick's medication was delivered to his doorstep by the local pharmacy. Three days after his dental surgery, a package arrived in the hands of a stunning delivery woman. Tessa reports she had long brown hair. Dick himself, however, claims to have perceived her as a "girl with black, black hair and large eyes very lovely and intense": a standard version of his fantasy of the dark-haired girl. Both Tessa and Philip's accounts agree that the delivery woman wore a gold pendant of a fish around her neck. In a 1975 letter, Dick writes,

"my entire experience was somehow triggered off . . . by the dark-haired stranger girl who came to my door in late February 1974 wearing the gold fish sign in necklace form, the sign of which had fascinated me so that I could not take my eyes off it, or off her. I had been expecting her most of my life: those black eyes, that black hair, and, around her neck, that gleaming gold chain of links culminating in the fish. I still remember saying to her, as in a daze, 'what is that you are wearing?' And the girl, touching it and saying, 'it's a sign that the early Christians used. My husband gave it to me'. And then she was gone."

According to Tessa, Dick already knew what the pendant was, as Christian fish signs were displayed in his neighborhood. If so, Dick had pretended not to know what the pendant meant, pretended to ask, and pretended to be edified by the delivery woman's answer. Tessa conjectures that the pretense was a low-key attempt at seduction. If Dick played dumb, maybe he could engage the woman in a longer conversation. His plan didn't work, though, and she left.

According to Tessa, Dick walked back to the bedroom, only to stop and cover his eyes. He was blinded by an overwhelming pink light. Some of Dick's accounts portray the light as a beam, others as more of a flash. Tessa believes the evening sun reflected off a silvery bumper sticker in the window, blinding Dick and triggering pink phosphene activity in his eyes. Dick sometimes endorses Tessa's version of the story, but elsewhere he says light reflected off the delivery woman's pendant blinded him. In both versions of the story, Dick collapsed and had a succession of visions. First came a series of abstract paintings, followed by philosophical ideas and engineering blueprints. In addition to this intellectual smorgasbord, Dick also saw ominous imagery. In one scene, he was trapped in a limousine in Vancouver. He was surrounded by anonymous men in black suits who interrogated him, asking him questions he could not understand. After the vision ended, Dick conjectured it was a memory awakened when the pink light struck him. He supposed he had been kidnapped two years earlier when in Canada, and brainwashed by the men in black. Perhaps the scene was a symbolic representation of his indoctrination at X-Kalay in Vancouver. Dick was afraid that, like the character in the then-popular film *The Manchurian Candidate*, he was hypnotically programmed to commit an act of wrongdoing whose nature he could not discern until it was too late. Or, he was being menaced by demons. For several weeks, Dick spent much of his time in bed semiconscious, experiencing visions.

Hot Dog Ovaltine Baptism

In March, Dick became terrified that his family was in danger of supernatural attack, and tried to protect his infant son by hastily baptizing him with a hot dog bun and cup of chocolate Ovaltine. In an interview with the BBC program *Arena*, Tessa describes the event: "Christopher's favorite meal for lunch was a hot dog, and Ovaltine. Phil put the hot dog aside because meat wouldn't be appropriate for a baptism, dipped his finger into the Ovaltine and drew a cross on Chris's forehead with it, and then he gave him a bite of the hot dog bun and a drink of the Ovaltine." Dick elaborates on the baptism in his autobiographical novel *VALIS*:

"Leaning toward him, I had whispered; 'In the name of the Son, the Father and the Holy Spirit.' No one heard me except Christopher. Now, as I wiped the warm chocolate from his hair, I inscribed the sign of the cross in his forehead. I had now baptized him and now I confirmed him ... Next I said to my son, "Your secret name, your Christian name, is—" And I told him what it was. ... Next, I took a bit of the bread from the hot dog bun and held it forth; my son— ... opened his mouth like a little bird, and I placed the bit of bread in it. ... For some reason it seemed essential—quite crucial—that he take no bite of the hot dog meat itself. Pork could not be eaten under these circumstances . . . As Christopher started to close his mouth to chew on the bit of bread, I presented him with the mug of warm chocolate. To my surprise— being so young he still drank normally from his bottle, never from a cup—he reached eagerly to take the mug; as he took it, lifted it to his lips and drank from it, I said, 'This is my blood and this is my body'."

Several characteristic qualities of Dick's divine madness appear in the story of the improvised baptism. For one thing, mundane features of everyday reality—in this case, a hot dog and a mug of hot chocolate—were increasingly granted an intense religious significance. Second, while Dick's religious experience drew upon established traditions, it creatively elaborated on them in an idiosyncratic way that can appear absurd. Although the baptism was Christian, the hot dog was pure Dick. The baptism is striking in its paradoxical combination of gravity and goofiness. It comes across as a deadpan joke, but was deadly serious. Dick literally feared that his son's immortal soul was in jeopardy and needed protection. That brings us to another aspect of 2-3-74: Dick started to feel like a protector standing against malign forces.

Revelations

In a letter to his friend Claudia Bush dated March 21, 1975, Dick describes the sequence of the unfolding religious experience in detail. He calls it "The Restorer of What Was Lost, The Mender of

What Was Broken." As I noted in Chapters 3 and 5, an important feature of Dick's psychology was dissociative estrangement from both the world and aspects of himself. In that sense, Dick's personality was "broken" into pieces. 2-3-74 provided an experience of intense wholeness that, for a time, mended these breaks. Dick writes that on March 16, "It appeared—in vivid fire, with shining colors and balanced patterns—and released me from every thrall, inner and outer." He seems to be referring to the visions he had while lying in bed, semiconscious. His emphasis on "fire" is consistent with typical reports of religious experiences. In many religious traditions, people touched by the divine often perceive it as flamelike. In the Bible, multiple scenes associate fire with the presence of God. In Eastern traditions such as Kundalini yoga, practitioners endeavor to awaken what is often referred to as an inner fire, a passionate energy that is believed to catalyze change. It is also common for religious experiences to include liberation from unhealthy psychological attachments or "thralls." Dick does not specify which "thralls" he has in mind, but often, spiritual liberation experiences release addictive cravings and other dependencies. Dick felt freed of the problems in living that had bound him.

On March 18, Dick writes in the letter to Bush, "It, from inside me, looked out and saw that the world did not compute, that I—and it—had been lied to. It denied the reality, and power, and authenticity, of the world, saying, 'this cannot exist; it cannot exist'." By "it," Dick elsewhere indicates, he refers to a divine presence that, he felt, had taken up residence inside him. The words "looked" and "saw" suggest the predominantly visual quality of Dick's mystical experience. Mystical revelations run the spectrum from emotional to tactile to auditory. Dick's particular revelation mostly involved a different way of *seeing*. The phrase "did not compute" also indicates that his experience had a cerebral quality. Although Dick's revelations were intense and fiery, they had a heady tone. They were a fire in the mind, not the heart or gut. They removed Dick from his immediate concerns, even his physical surroundings. The world did not compute.

On March 20 he writes:

> "It seized me entirely, lifting me from the limitations of the space-time matrix; it mastered me as, at the same instant, I knew that the world around me was cardboard, a fake. Through its power I saw suddenly the universe as it was; through its power of perception I saw what really existed, and through its power of no-thought decision, I acted to free myself. It took on in battle, as a champion of all human spirits in thrall, every evil, every Iron Imprisoning thing."

In this passage, Dick says that he was both "seized" and "mastered" by the divine presence that he formerly felt had been residing within him and looking out at the world. The mystical way of seeing into which Dick was initiated suddenly became more firmly secured in his mind. Now, it was not merely that the world "did not compute," but that Dick now "saw suddenly the universe as it was." Dick was first liberated from attachments, then, it appears, from the world itself. Out of the negation of reality as Dick had formerly seen it, a more fundamental truth emerged. The detection of a lie had given way to perception of the truth. Dick emphasizes the "power of perception," indicating again that perception was a central feature of his religious experience. He also refers to a "power of no-thought decision." It is not immediately clear what Dick means here, but he might be referring to a process of making decisions based on perception rather than thought. For example, if one perceives oneself to be trapped in a fake world, the decision to free oneself follows naturally. To see the trap is to decide to be free of it.

Another emerging quality of Dick's revelation was that it had a combative tone. Dick perceived "Imprisoning thing[s]" as evil, and liberation as good. To be liberated, for Dick, was also to be enlisted into the battle against imprisoning things. It was to join a spiritual revolution. Not only that, but Dick was not to be merely a foot soldier in the revolution but its "champion." Becoming the champion of all beings must have provided a massive boost to Dick's self-esteem. He was no longer an impoverished genre writer who could barely support his family, but the guiding light of worldwide spiritual liberation.

From March 20 until July, Dick writes,

> "it . . . knew how to give ceaseless battle, to defeat the tyranny which had entered by slow degrees our free world; our pure world; it fought and destroyed tirelessly each and every one of them, and saw them all clearly, with dislike; its love was for justice and truth beyond everything else."

One feature that stands out in this passage is the sustained energy that 2-3-74 provided. Dick often had long periods of being bedridden, unable to work or even attend to daily tasks. 2-3-74 lent Dick a font of "tireless" passion that felt inexhaustible. It was better than amphetamines. Another theme is *purity*. Dick felt himself to be fighting for pure justice and truth. He now saw the world as contaminated with falsehood and injustice. Notably, the March 20 aspect of his revelation had a historical character. The world was not only revealed to be a falsehood, but the historical process of contamination by which that falsehood had come to hide the truth was also unveiled.

Zebra

Dick increasingly detected a spiritual presence in his physical environment. He noticed movement out of the corner of his eye and caught glimpses of an entity surreptitiously observing him and Tessa. It camouflaged itself so as to blend in with any surrounding, hence Dick's name for it: Zebra. In an *Exegesis* entry describing Zebra, he writes "it (Zebra) can enter anything, animate or inanimate; in the latter it takes volitional control of causal processes—mimesis, mimicry, camouflage." Sometimes, Zebra blended into inanimate objects, sometimes into groups of people. Dick told Tessa that the entity had a third eye in the middle of its forehead, but it remained closed. If the entity opened its third eye, Dick felt, its enemies would detect and kill it. Dick became obsessed with Zebra, and characterized it variously as a false god, a humanoid life form, Christ, and the Holy Spirit. He noted that Zebra was paranoia turned inside out. Whereas paranoia fills one's mind with fears of hidden and malign observers, Zebra was a hidden benign observer. It watched with love.

In *Exegesis* entries, Dick details the methods of camouflage employed by Zebra. Zebra not only conceals itself but also prevents Dick from fully grasping his own identity. "So any and all ideas I get as to my identity, nature, purpose and origin is just scatter, random flak, each idea as real and unreal as the next; like white noise." The closer he gets to his true identity, the fuzzier and more conflicted Dick's thinking becomes. Even worse, his ideas about his identity are themselves camouflage. As Dick continues to generate ideas about who he is, he is like a cuttlefish emitting ink. The ideas conceal, rather than reveal. Zebra won't even allow Dick to fully nail down his narrative of 2-3-74, which he regularly revises: "I can't give the same account twice re 74, re Zebra and re myself." Zebra permeates Dick's existence so thoroughly that his own attempts to understand Zebra's manifestations are infected by Zebra's camouflaging process. The net result is an infinite paradoxical flux that shows up both in Dick's spiritual journey and his efforts to grasp it. "This suggests," Dick writes, "that I and the life form Zebra are one." Zebra, perhaps, is Dick looking into a mirror. Or Dick is Zebra looking into a mirror.

Mercury

Later, as Zebra entered more fully into Dick's awareness, he perceived it as "like red-and-gold shining mercury, it flowed off and disappeared almost as soon as I spied it." Here, Dick implies that the "flowing" mercury-like quality he attributes to the red-and-gold spectacle was related to how he looked at it. It seemed to "flow" because it vanished when he gazed squarely at it. Yet in other writings, Dick indicates that the flowing quality of what he saw was actually independent of how he looked at it.

For example, he writes he saw "gold and red outside, like liquid fire" or "shiny fire" and "red and gold living threads of activity in the outside world." The threads of liquid fire appeared to have "enormous mass" and were "capable of terrific velocity." In these remarks, Dick seems to be saying that he saw powerful streams of red-and-gold–colored energy weaving their way through his environment, a bit like eels might weave their way through a coral reef. Perhaps Dick's red-and-gold vision was, so to speak, meta-mercurial—both a perception of a dynamic flow and a dynamic flow of perception. He saw living threads of activity from the perspective of *being* a living thread of activity. *What* he saw and *how* he saw it matched up.

He further describes the mercury entity as akin to "over-amped (valent) red phospers in the tube gun (cathode tube) of a TV set." The red color he saw glowed, like the cathode tube of an old TV set. Dick also refers to his vision as that of "a gold and red illuminated-letter like plasmatic entity from the future, arranging bits and pieces here: arranging what time drove forward." Dick elaborates: "It was/is alive. It had a certain small power or energy, and great wisdom. It was/is holy. It not only was visible around me but evidently this is the same energy which entered me. It was both inside and out." The gold and red colors are recurrent motifs in 2-3-74, and in Christian thought are liturgical colors believed to symbolize the presence of God. On the other hand, Dick's remark that the divine energy was both inside and outside him is perhaps more consistent with nondual religious traditions such as Advaita Vedanta. Practitioners of nondual traditions typically experience a dissolution of dichotomous boundaries such as inner/outer and self/other, perceiving the world is an undifferentiated wholeness. Dick writes that he saw the red-and-gold "entity" looking from inside him and seeing itself outside. He seems to have experienced it as an energetic bridge that linked him profoundly with the world. The red-and-gold vision, then, had both Christian and nondual features.

It is challenging, though, to determine what Dick means when he refers to Zebra as "illuminated-letter like." Perhaps Dick means to refer to the artistic style of the red-and-gold lettering characteristic of so-called "illuminated" medieval religious texts. It may be most consistent with Dick's account to conclude he had transient visions of red-and-gold streams of active energy that struck him as having an intensely meaningful character and, as a result, felt like messages. Sometimes they took the shape of actual letters, and sometimes not. Did he see any letter in particular? Occasionally, he saw the word "Felix," in the sense of its Latin meaning of "happy." Dick took "Felix" to be a word expressing God's love. Years after 2-3-74, Dick also claims that in 1979 he had a hypnogogic vision of the letters YHWH in gold and red. However, Dick's other descriptions of the red and gold colors indicate that the visions of actual letters were rare.

Dick also attributes a temporal quality to the red-and-gold energy. It felt to him as if the energy both portended future possibilities and was also coming back at him from the future. The energy had a creative, world-shaping quality to it. Dick says that he saw the energy rearranging the world in order to give birth to a fresh future. Just as it was transforming him from the inside, so too was it transforming the world outside of him. His future was a double of the future of the world.

The Golden Rectangle

Among the forms Dick saw was the Golden Rectangle, a geometric figure discovered by ancient Greek mathematicians and popular in ancient architecture. The distinctive feature of the Golden Rectangle is that when a square shape is removed from it, a smaller version of the rectangle of the same ratio is left over. The Golden Rectangle, then, can be infinitely reduced to progressively smaller versions of itself by removing squares. It is believed to be aesthetically pleasing, and Dick says it was calming to him.

Dick first appears to have seen the Golden Rectangle as an abstract figure, then later embodied in his surrounding environment. In one repeated vision, he saw the Golden Rectangle as a "pylon or arch-like doorway with the Greek water and nighttime island scene, so beautiful and peaceful on the other side." While he had the vision during the day, the world Dick saw was at night. He elaborates that he heard "bells and the lady singing . . . and the golden rectangle doorway with the sea and figure beyond, and the moonlight." He characterizes what he saw through the doorway as a "lovely quiet peaceful world on the other side, waiting." Dick took the rectangle archway vision to be a perception of a spiritual world that was immanent in his familiar everyday surroundings. The vision was, for him, filled with meaning, and he felt it "explained everything" in a way that could not be articulated. Dick got a glimpse of paradise.

The Xerox Missive

Like the Golden Rectangle, some of Dick's visions were peaceful. Yet, others had a combative quality. Consistent with the combative aspects of Dick's revelations, his paranoia remained prominent off and on throughout 2-3-74. He feared his February vision of men in black meant they had brainwashed him to self-destruct. Soon after the blast of pink light, Dick expected to receive a letter that would activate a posthypnotic suggestion resulting in his death. Although no such letter materialized, Dick did get an odd piece of mail ambiguous enough to be woven into his fears. In late February or early March, an envelope arrived with no name on its return address, postmarked Osterreich (German for Austria). According to Tessa, it contained a Xerox copy of a review of a book about the downfall of American capitalism. Dick asked Tessa to read him the letter but not let him see it, presumably to prevent the activation of the fatal posthypnotic suggestion he anticipated. Tessa does not recall what book was reviewed, but specific words throughout the review were underlined. These included what Dick called "die words" like "destruction," "annihilation," and "decomposition." He later referred to the copied book review as the Xerox Missive, and speculated that it might be a KGB attempt to recruit him, or alternatively an FBI effort to test his loyalty. Dick called the FBI and the local police, informing them he was a dangerous machine and should be incarcerated. They ignored him. For several months, Dick wrote to the FBI declaring his loyalty to the United States. He "mailed" his letters by dropping them into a garbage dumpster in an alley near his apartment. If the FBI was monitoring Dick, he believed, its agents should be able to detect and retrieve the letters. If, on the other hand, the FBI was not monitoring him, no harm done.

Some might contend that the Xerox Missive proves 2-3-74 was a paranoid episode. I disagree. As I discussed in the last two chapters, Dick was severely paranoid for many years prior to 2-3-74. *Yes*, the Xerox Missive was a paranoid event, *but* Dick's paranoia predated 2-3-74. It was already there. That said, it is possible that Dick's lifelong fears of annihilation were amplified by the transformation of his identity that occurred during 2-3-74. Radical changes of identity require the loss of an old identity, and that loss can be felt as an annihilating destruction of the self. Fears of self-loss are often characteristic of mystical experience, and can take paranoid forms. The Xerox Missive, perhaps, displays the destructive side of 2-3-74, a necessary complement to its creative side. For a new self to arise, an old self must die. Sometimes, the death of Dick's old self felt liberating, and at other times it was terrifying.

Plasmate Possession

Dick felt that a higher entity had guided his reaction to the Xerox Missive—specifically, the spirit of a man named Thomas whom Dick thought was an ancient Christian martyr from the first century. Thomas, Dick felt, was a resident of tyrannical Rome.

While inhabited by the personality of Thomas, Dick perceived the world through two viewpoints divorced in time. From Thomas's perspective, American capitalism was a variation of Roman enslavement. Dick had a dream in which he heard a reference to Thomas: "there's someone else inside my head and he's not living in this century." Thomas was, according to Dick, a millenarian and revolutionary idealist. He hoped to overthrow the tyranny of Rome to clear the way for a new world of freedom and justice. A more mundane characteristic of Thomas was an aversion to lead and aerosol sprays. Why lead and aerosol? I would conjecture that the lead and aerosol aversion was an early manifestation of the ecological dimension of Dick's spirituality, which would later become more dramatic in his visions of Tagore, a world savior, which I will discuss in the next chapter.

Dick believed Thomas communed with him through a symbiotic organism he called a *plasmate*. He describes plasmates as entities made of living energy that invade the human body through the optic nerve. The pink light that struck Dick, he supposed, was the energy of the plasmate entering his eyes. He speculated that the red-and-gold energy of his visions was also plasmate energy. According to Dick's theories, plasmates mate with humans (hence the term plas-"mate") by impregnating the human brain and reproducing themselves as pure information. Dick witnessed plasmates in visions while overwhelmed by anxiety. In one terrifying vision that lasted for hours, he saw "frightening vortexes [sic] of light" that "spun round and around, and moved away at incredible speed." Dick's thoughts joined with the vortexes of light, and he felt he was traveling at the speed of light. Later, Dick saw a ball of blue light that flitted around his bedroom and dove into his head. He named the ball "Firebright," and construed it as a version of the plasmate that had symbiotically joined with him and enabled him to communicate with Thomas. In addition to Thomas, Dick claimed to hold plasmate-facilitated communication with Francis Bacon, St. Augustine, Simon Magus, and other prominent figures from religious history. Occasionally, the experience took on a paranoid character and he feared the plasmate was a chip implanted in his head by the KGB, but most of the time, it seemed benevolent.

Guidance from the Other Side

Dick felt one of the personages telepathically communicating with him was his deceased friend and mentor, James Pike. I mentioned earlier that in the 1960s Dick had transcribed a séance in which Pike attempted to communicate with the spirit of his deceased son. In August 1969, Pike died of exposure during a visit to Israel. He and his wife were gathering material for a book about the historical Jesus. The plan was that they would follow the path of Jesus's footsteps. They rented a car in Bethlehem and drove out into the desert, planning to explore the wilderness where Jesus was said to have been tempted by the Devil. The wheels of their car got stuck, and Pike and his wife had to try and escape the desert on foot. After a few hours of walking, Pike collapsed, unable to proceed further. His wife was able to reach help, but by the time she returned, Pike was dead.

Just as Pike believed he came into contact with his deceased son during the séances Dick had attended, Dick felt he had encountered the deceased James Pike. Pike was coming through from the Other Side. Dick received "floods of information, night after night, about the religions of the Antique World" on which Pike was an expert, and read books he believed Pike would read. When he closed his eyes, images of photographs and writing familiar to Pike appeared. Pike's spirit silently instructed him on mundane issues such as how to trim his beard or which alcoholic beverages to consume. According to Pike's spirit, beer was okay, whereas hard liquor was forbidden. It also asked Dick to clip his nose hair. He says Pike's spirit helped him make more money from his writing than ever before. Detecting discrepancies between the royalty checks he received and the sales of his books, he demanded an audit from one of his publishers, Doubleday. He also renegotiated his contract with his literary agency, the Meredith Agency, insisting they follow up on royalties Ace Books owed him for previous book sales. As a result, Dick received over $3,000 in back royalties, which adjusted for inflation would today equate to approximately $17,000. Dick also resolved his IRS crisis by arranging a payment plan. Dick sometimes felt as if he and Pike had switched places, as if Pike was alive and Dick was dead. This spin on Dick's reality had it that his entire life after Pike's death was an illusion, a false timeline. Anomalies in Dick's perception, such as his hallucinations, led him to suspect that his environment was a fabrication that papered over the basic reality that he was dead while Pike was alive. Previously, I mentioned that Dick saw Pike as a benign double, a better self. Dick's relationship to his deceased friend increasingly resembled his attitude toward his dead twin. Like Jane, Pike was a dead double with whom Dick felt interchangeable.

Sophia and the AI Voice

At times, however, Dick sensed the personality guiding him was not Pike at all, but a divine woman. During Dick's semiconscious reveries, the so-called AI voice from his high school physics exam returned to provide advice. Sometimes her responses sounded like gibberish. Dick asked the AI voice who she was, and she replied "Sadassa Ulna." When he asked where she was, she said she had an envelope on a nearby desk whose address read "Portuguese States of America." She gave cryptic advice like "you have to put your slippers on to walk toward the dawn." Dick took this utterance to be a complex way of providing maternal reassurance. He writes in the *Exegesis*:

> " 'You have to put your slippers on' is what your mama says to you . . . at night before you go to bed, to hear the story she is going to tell you; it suggests safety . . . put your slippers on . . . to keep your feet warm, which could be deciphered as, 'You must not have cold feet', which . . . means, 'Don't be scared; you must not be scared or you can't walk toward the Dawn', which itself is a metaphor for 'moving toward enlightenment'."

As in his high school physics exam, the AI voice functioned to alleviate Dick's fear. It calmed him down, while also promising special access to wisdom.

Dick felt 2-3-74 "put me in touch with [the eternal feminine] in me"—*Sophia*, a figure from Gnostic theology. Gnosticism was an ancient heretical version of Christianity that considered the world to be a simulacrum created by a false god known as the *demiurge*. Gnostics believed that to get beyond the false world and into the real world, one had to have a special immediate knowledge of God and reality called *gnosis*. *Gnosis* was said to be distinct from faith in that it is based on direct mystical experience rather than ideological belief. For the Gnostic, the primary function of Jesus Christ was to bring *gnosis* that would free the Gnostic from the false reality in which he or she was imprisoned. For the ancient Gnostic, reality is like the fake world depicted in movies like *The Matrix*, except that it is not fashioned by malicious computers but by a false deity. In principle, Gnosticism is the reverse of organized Christianity: rather than indoctrinating the adherent into a belief system, it aims to free him or her by granting direct access to mystical experiences that render religious ideology superfluous.

In Gnostic mythology, Sophia is the bride of Christ and is bonded with him as part of a spiritual pair. One version of the myth has it that Sophia becomes entranced by the reflected light of the spiritual world that is cast on the material world, and leaves Christ for the material world in order to seize and further duplicate this light. She tries to give life to inert matter, but is only partially successful because her act of life giving is performed without the help of her consort. The end result is the birth of the false god known as the demiurge, who proceeds to erect an inherently flawed cosmos. However, Gnosticism claims that because of Sophia's involvement in the creation of human beings, every human being has a spark of Sophia within, a spark that constitutes the soul. Gnostic stories about Sophia provided one source of inspiration for Jung's famous concept of the *anima*, a female component of the male mind that provides an interface linking the individual ego with the Collective Unconscious. According to Jung, the shape the anima takes in a man's mental life is related to the level of integration in his personality. Jung associates Sophia with the highest achievement of personality integration and, therefore, wisdom. Dick was as familiar with Jungian psychology as he was with Gnosticism, and was well aware his fascination with Sophia connected with Jungian theory.

Consistent with both Jungian theory and Gnostic mythology, Dick felt there was an essential feminine part of him that was linked with divine wisdom. Dick characterized Sophia as compassionate, too, an internal center of harmony and calm. The link between Dick's vision of Sophia and his deceased twin sister was obvious to him: maybe, he conjectured, Sophia appeared because he was in spiritual "symbiosis" to his dead sister, and therefore psychically linked to her. He writes: "The AI voice is my imaginary playmate, my sister, evolved out of my childhood . . . fantasies." Dick's feelings about his twin sister were both Gnostic theology revealed and Jungian theory concretely realized. As he puts it, "But my search in this world, in all worlds, is for my sister, my female counterpart whom I have lost—been separated from. Still, she exists, and finally I will be reunited with her. She is very close to me as the AI voice."

The Empire Never Ended

When Dick was a child, he had a recurring nightmare in which he anxiously rifled through piles of science fiction magazines searching for a short story entitled "The Empire Never Ended." In the dream, Dick was excited to find the story, but then terrified of what it might contain. Despite his terror, he could not stop searching. With each new iteration of the nightmare, Dick came ever closer to uncovering the frightening unknown narrative. When he grew up, he stopped having the nightmare, but the terrifying latent story of the Empire lurked on, incubating in a corner of Dick's mind for years, and then surfaced during 2-3-74.

In March of 1974, Dick began having visions of scenes of the ancient Roman Empire superimposed over his environment. In a letter to Claudia Bush, he writes, "in March I looked around and saw *Rome! Rome everywhere*! Power and force, stone walls, iron bars . . . I pierced the veil, so to speak, and saw my society exactly as it was . . . which is . . . like Rome was . . . It was a dreadful sight: a slave state, like Gulag." During a trip to the market, Tessa and Philip passed a daycare center where children played in a fenced-in yard. At least, that's what Tessa saw. To Philip, the daycare center appeared to be an ancient Roman prison. Where there was a chain-link fence, Dick saw iron bars, and where there were children playing, Philip saw weeping Christian martyrs prepared to be fed to lions. During other walks in the neighborhood, Dick saw pedestrians dressed in Roman military uniforms, stone walls, and iron bars on windows of apartments. "I hadn't gone back in time," Dick writes to Bush, "but in a sense Rome had come forward, by insidious and sly degrees, under new names, hidden by the flak talk and phony obscurations, at last into our world again." Dick believed his visions meant the modern world was an illusion and he was actually living in ancient Rome. He started to feel time must have stopped centuries ago, and humanity was frozen in the year 70 A.D., the year the temple of Jerusalem was destroyed by a

Roman siege. Dick called this arrest in the movement of time "the Black Iron Prison."

Dick elaborates, in the *Exegesis*, that there was included in the experience a sense that Rome was after *him*, in particular:

> "I was . . . aware . . . of my own identity standing in opposition to it; hence its hostility toward me—the scurrying of its agents were specifically hostile toward me, and I had to work in stealth, e.g. to baptize Christopher et al . . . I was a member of a secret group which Rome was dedicated to destroy; this made me part of the Fish sign secret society, killed on identification and disclosure."

In this passage, it becomes clear that major aspects of 2-3-74 were thematically structured around the fish sign. By flashing Dick the fish sign, the dark-haired delivery girl placed him in the role of a secret Christian. As such, Dick *had* to be hiding from somebody, and that somebody, for ancient Christians, had been ancient Rome. It made sense, then, that as Dick's identity shifted, so too would his perception of his surroundings.

Other aspects of 2-3-74 seem unrelated to the fish sign. Dick had visions of tiny humanoid extraterrestrials who, he said, were time travelers who had come to liberate humanity from the Black Iron Prison. Dick witnessed these creatures enter his home by means of a bright pink rectangular portal that appeared on his bedroom wall. It was the Golden Rectangle again, made of pink light. Dick told his wife the extraterrestrials had massive heads and thin slits for mouths. She looked for them, and sometimes felt she could just barely detect them out of the corner of her eye.

They were silent, communicating with Dick telepathically. The time travelers said they had tried, and failed, to prevent the assassinations of John Kennedy, Robert Kennedy, and Che Guevara. According to the hallucinatory time travelers, John and Robert Kennedy's assassins, the CIA, and the Nixon administration were complicit in maintaining the dominance of the Roman Empire hidden beneath the veneer of the modern world. Nixon, himself, was the emperor of Rome. As Dick put it, he saw an "apocalyptic reality underlying our reality." In a 1981 interview, Dick reports that it was as if a veil had been removed from the world and he was able to see it as it truly was.

In a September 1974 letter to Ursula Le Guin, Dick elaborates: "The spirit which filled me starting in March was primarily rooted in these realities: justice, truth, and freedom ... The spirit when he arrived here looked around, saw Richard Nixon and those creatures, and was so wrath-filled that he never stopped writing letters to Washington until Nixon was out." Dick sent letter after letter to Congress identifying the deceptions in Nixon's transcripts and detailing legal options for ousting him. It appears he literally believed his letters were instrumental in Nixon's impeachment, and later conjectured that the defeat of Nixon (as a representative of the Black Iron Prison) was a chief purpose of his spiritual experience. Dick felt that divine forces had worked through him to impeach Nixon. Dick continues in the letter,

"This spirit, very Elijah-like ... confuted the lies of the world with enormous insight into them; he used legal terms I don't generally use. You wouldn't believe his animosity toward the tyrannies both here and in the USSR; he saw them as twin horns of the same evil entity—one vast worldwide state whose basic nature was clear to him as being one of slavery, a continuation of Rome itself. And he was a foe to that, above all; he saw Caesar once more, and himself pitted against that . . ."

It becomes clearer what Dick had meant when he earlier said that the spirit filling him was rooted in "justice, truth, and freedom." As he describes it, the alien "personality" was highly attuned to aspects of tyranny based on deception. To fight against tyranny was to fight for truth.

Dick goes on to talk about time travel: "What perhaps is involved here is time travel. The ability by someone, or several someones, far back in the past (circa 600 B.C.) to travel forward through to our period, by large leaps, surfacing in one of us . . ." The word "perhaps" indicates that the time-travel idea is more of a theory *about* 2-3-74 than a direct experience that emerged at that time. As part of its phenomenology, 2-3-74 had paradoxical temporal features that contradicted the everyday experience of time. Dick felt inhabited by something ancient, and was attuned to aspects of his environment reflecting old patterns of tyranny dating back to ancient Rome. *Time* was certainly a central aspect of Dick's direct experience of 2-3-74, but time *travel*, per se, appears to be a theory he added to it.

Strawberry Transmission

To prove the validity of his revelations, Dick often makes reference to a crisis in which the pink light warned him that his infant son Chris had a dire medical condition. In August of 1974, Dick injured his shoulder by throwing a seashell during an argument with Tessa. Recovering from surgery, he awoke to the sound of his son babbling, and heard it as a series of pleas spoken in Aramaic. "Eloi, Eloi, lama sabachthani," he heard, a famous utterance of Christ during the crucifixion, which is translated as "My God, my God, why have you forsaken me?"

Dick's and Tessa's versions of the rest of the story differ. His is the more colorful. In Dick's version, he was listening to the Beatles song "Strawberry Fields Forever" with his eyes shut. Hearing a line from the song about going through life with one's eyes closed, he stood up and opened his eyes, at which point he was blinded by light from a window. Closing his eyes again, Dick had a vision of "strange strawberry ice cream pink" and the lyrics of the song transformed into a statement of warning: "Your son has an undiagnosed right inguinal hernia. The hydrocele has burst, and it has descended into the scrotal sac. He requires immediate attention, or will soon die." Dick and his wife rushed their son to a physician, who scheduled him for an emergency operation.

What Dick leaves out of the story is that his wife suspected their son had a hernia long before Dick's strawberry revelation. Tessa's version has it that one day, while she was cooking breakfast, Dick awoke from a nap. He acted, she writes, as if in a "hypnotic trance." He called to Tessa to get the doctor, exclaiming that God's voice had come through the bedside radio and told him that their baby had an undiagnosed hernia and could die. Whereas in Dick's version Tessa immediately took their son to the family doctor, she says it was several days before she did so. Also, in Tessa's version, the family doctor referred her to a specialist. It was the specialist, not the family doctor, who confirmed the diagnosis.

The specialist said the infant had indeed been at risk of strangulation if the hernia had been left untreated. That said, the operation did not actually take place until October. If we take Tessa's story as the more accurate version, it seems the strawberry revelation worked in the same way as Dick's Eureka moment during his high school physics final, as I discussed in Chapter 4. Like the voice Dick heard during the physics exam, the voice from over the radio connected him to vital information he already had. Just as Dick already knew Archimedes' principle but needed the AI voice to remind him of it, he already knew his son had a hernia but needed God's voice to verify it. Both voices relayed messages from Dick to himself, using the channel of dissociation.

Pike's silent instructions to Dick on how to trim his beard, as well as Sophia's cryptic reassurances, can be understood similarly. Indeed, all Dick's experiences of mystical guidance during 2-3-74 repeat the dissociative process from the physics exam. All of the figures guiding Dick—Thomas, Pike, Sophia, Zebra—reminded him of information he already should have known, like how to trim his beard and how to conduct his business. These mystical personages provided dissociative access to wisdom Dick already possessed. They were avatars of psychological wholeness. Put aside the drama, and what is left is Dick becoming one with himself by telling himself what he already knew.

The Exegesis Begins

After August of 1974, Dick's religious experiences decreased in frequency and intensity. He still occasionally had mystical experiences, but these no longer dominated the entire world of his subjective experience as they had during 2-3-74. There were moments when he felt himself to be in contact with other-worldly forces, but he no longer saw his post office as an outpost of the Roman Empire. Nevertheless, Dick's mind remained intellectually fixed on 2-3-74 throughout the rest of his life. He was obsessed, much as he had been with the phantom burglary. He spun out theory after theory of what his visions and revelations meant, drawing from religious literature, philosophy, psychoanalysis, medicine, and science fiction. He spent hours each night presenting his latest theory of 2-3-74 to groups of his friends. Apparently, Dick's expositions were entertaining enough to keep people listening. Most people couldn't tell if Dick had had a mental breakdown or whether he was just fooling around. One acquaintance, Thomas Disch, recalled that Dick "translate[ed] every imagined thing into a belief or a suspended belief." On top of the actual experiences Dick had in 2-3-74, he placed layers upon layers of intellectual exposition and conjecture. The memory of 2-3-74, Dick later wrote, slid away from him, and he became unable to recall it as it really happened. Reading Dick's *Exegesis*, one may begin to suspect what is important is less 2-3-74 than the process of endlessly obsessing over the meaning of 2-3-74. Figuring out 2-3-74 was about the journey, not the destination. The *Exegesis* never ended.

8 | THE *EXEGESIS*
LIVING INFORMATION

A key theme of the *Exegesis* is Dick's pop philosophical concept of *living information*. To Dick, his spiritual revelations were literally a form of life. He theorized that during his mystical awakening of 2-3-74, his brain was literally impregnated with a self-replicating ancient organism that had lain dormant since biblical times. Perhaps, Dick conjectured, an ancient Christian scroll James Pike uncovered in Israel had housed an information-based life form that infected Pike and was then transferred from him to Dick. Dick's books, his stories, and even the *Exegesis* itself were the offspring of this organism. The organism was God, or at least an aspect of God, in the process of redeeming the world by absorbing it into itself. It was a kind of spiritual terraforming. God was transforming the irrational world into a rational universe fit for humans. Animated by the spirit of God, Dick's writings both disclosed and performed this process of spiritual transformation. They revealed the insane and illusory nature of reality while hinting at the divine intervention that promised to restore it to rationality. By uncovering this spiritual truth, Dick made the world more intelligible, thereby contributing to the process of redemption. In other words, Dick believed that with every book, every story, every new page of his journal, he quite literally saved the world.

Because Dick felt that sparks of God were alive within his writings, he had to treat these as sacred objects of worship. Each word that his typewriter stamped out was alit with the Divine. Each story was its own Bible, requiring its own religious interpretation. Much of the *Exegesis* is mystical interpretation of Dick's own science fiction stories. Dick categorizes his books and stories by the nature of the mystical knowledge they reveal. He reads stories such as "The Electric Ant" and "The Imposter" as divine messages disclosing the deceitful nature of reality. By contrast, novels in which a spurious reality is penetrated by an ultimate rescuer, such as *Ubik* and *A Maze of Death*, are categorized as tales of the coming of God. Naturally, the *Exegesis* itself is not exempt from its own exegetical activity. Sometimes, the *Exegesis* folds back upon itself, as Dick analyzes the bits of divine information embedded in his prior journal entries. Because of its circular self-referential process, the *Exegesis* not only reinterprets Dick's prior writings, but continually generates additional material for Dick to interpret as it rolls along. The *Exegesis* is both text and commentary, and is always one step ahead of itself. The *Exegesis* also became a primary inspiration for Dick's published writing, giving rise to Dick's last three novels, *VALIS, The Divine Invasion*, and *The Transmigration of Timothy Archer.*

In fact, the self-generating nature of the *Exegesis* fits one definition of life endorsed by biologists: *autopoiesis*. According to Francisco Varela and Humberto Maturana, the central feature of living systems is that they are self-maintaining or "autopoietic." Living systems regenerate and transform themselves; this feature distinguishes them from machines. Although Dick does not appear to have been familiar with the work of Varela and

Maturana, their views provide a scientific basis for his claims about living information. If all self-generating systems are by definition alive, and the *Exegesis* is a self-generating system, then it is by definition alive. One can take this line of reasoning further: if the present chapter is itself an offspring of the *Exegesis*, the words you read at this moment would have to be alive, breathing.

However, since all texts are to some extent self-generating, the next logical step would be to recognize all text as a form of life. When we walk down the library aisle, we walk not through stacks of inert bound paper, but through hives of living creatures ready to impregnate us with informational offspring. Not only books, but street signs, menus, and traffic tickets would have to be living entities. All writing would teem with life. If Dick had taken his beliefs that far, it would present a problem, because then his writing would no longer appear the least bit special. His *Exegesis* would be merely a specimen of the type of organism referred to as the "journal."

For Dick to maintain that the *Exegesis* has a mystical distinction from other texts, provenance was critical. This is one of several reasons why Dick maintains 2-3-74 as a central theme throughout the *Exegesis*. 2-3-74 provides the *Exegesis* with an origin story that infuses it with meaning. It anchors the *Exegesis* in a mystical experience that functions to provide religious authority to the text. 2-3-74 is proof of life in the *Exegesis*. On the other hand, the *Exegesis* also endeavors to legitimize 2-3-74 as something more credible than mental illness. When Dick provides mountains of references to religious and philosophical traditions, it is evident he is trying to demonstrate that his mystical experiences are of universal significance, rather than the quirky sputterings of a broken brain. A careful reading shows that Dick is largely successful in this effort. After perusing his descriptions of relevant aspects of Neoplatonism, Buddhism, Gnosticism, and Hinduism, it is impossible to deny their affinities to 2-3-74. Nevertheless, Dick undermines his credibility when he rewrites 2-3-74 in light of those traditions, revising elements of his experience to match whatever religious teaching he is flirting with at any particular time. Dick's main bodies of reference in this respect were the *Encyclopedia Britannica* and Paul Edwards' *Encyclopedia of Philosophy*, and his reliance on encyclopedias shows. One can see him comparing 2-3-74 with each new encyclopedia entry he reads, creatively reinterpreting his experience each time. With each revision of 2-3-74, the credibility of Dick's analysis fades and 2-3-74 appears more and more like whatever Dick needs it to be at any given moment. 2-3-74 is the *Exegesis'* MacGuffin.

On the other hand, it could also be argued that the *Exegesis'* status as living information requires that there be recurrent autopoietic revisions of 2-3-74. Just as the 2-3-74 proves that the *Exegesis* is alive by establishing its point of birth, the ongoing reinventions of 2-3-74 prove the continuing autopoietic life of Dick's experience. 2-3-74 was not hypostatized into an inert factual account of What Really Happened Then, but continually regenerated into new forms. Its life carried forward with each retelling. Indeed, it would be consistent with Dick's Teilhardian philosophy to argue that 2-3-74 was perfected further with each subsequent revision. Rationality and order, to Dick, increase over time. Dick saw time as a conflict between entropic and anti-entropic forces. Left to itself, time naturally flows toward greater disorder or entropy. However, Dick proposes, God provides a counterforce toward increased order or "negentropy." Dick believed that the spirit of God works backward in time, configuring past events retroactively into more and more meaningful and orderly arrangements. Events that seem irrational when they initially happen are later reconfigured into more rational shapes as God's spirit plunges back in time to reach them. From this angle, God is a spiritual time traveler, moving through history to reshape past realities to fit a future utopia of spiritual perfection, which Dick called the Palm Tree Garden. It is no surprise Dick compares his God to a fiction writer who edits and re-edits old material to fit new storylines and plot points. Dick even takes the comparison a step further into what may seem like madness: he proposes that his own writing is a microcosm of God's re-editing of reality, and therefore that he himself is a version of God. Although grandiose, Dick's claim to godhood makes sense of his friends' reports that he lost himself in his writing so deeply that he would often emerge from his study believing he was one of his characters. After 2-3-74, Dick's subjective experience of his creative process had become so profound that it felt like he was reconfiguring the world. Writing was not merely a crafting of stories about reality, but a reworking of reality itself. While Dick wrote, he was God and God was he. As in the Beetle Satori discussed in Chapter 3, Dick's identification with God made the microcosm one with the macrocosm. As Dick reworked his stories and theories into greater perfection, God reworked the world into greater rationality. It was all the same thing.

To be sure, the notion of God as fiction writer is precarious, as it implies God may be untrustworthy. And in fact, sometimes Dick verges on portraying God as a cosmic bullshit artist orchestrating a spiritual conspiracy. God, Dick has it, is a master of camouflage, taking on the forms of inanimate objects in order to incorporate them into its divine body. That desk, that couch, that microwave oven, could be God in disguise. To highlight God's camouflage, Dick sometimes equates God with Zebra. Expanding on his experiences from 2-3-74, Dick describes Zebra as a gigantic disguised entity covering vast distances in space and time. One might assume that because Zebra is cloaked, it must be malevolent. After all, who would wear a mask but a criminal? Indeed, in Dick's older writings, the spurious nature of reality is a clue that the world is fabricated by a malign creature. Although this paranoid theme continues to crop up in the *Exegesis*, it is leavened by a more optimistic view in which God's illusions are benign. The latter view, which Dick calls the Zebra Principle, seems to have emerged out of 2-3-74, and represents a shift in Dick's attitude.

Zebra

The Zebra Principle turns Dick's paranoia inside out. According to it, human beings are deceived for our own good. Rather than simulating reality to deceive humans, Zebra incorporates reality into itself in order to make it more real. Rather than imprisoning human beings in a false world, Zebra emancipates us by reweaving a hidebound reality into fresh shapes. Rather than concealing our true identities from us, Zebra reconstitutes identity itself. Dick compares Zebra to an insect that mimics our reality and then sheds it like a cocoon in order to give birth to a paradisiacal world. The sufferings of living beings are birth pangs that herald the Palm Tree Garden.

But Dick's newfound trust in Zebra only goes so far. As he continues pondering the nature of Zebra, he recalls the eerie visions of 2-3-74 in which he saw small three-eyed alien creatures creeping into his bedroom through a portal. Dick wonders if perhaps the deceptive behavior of Zebra implies that the spurious nature of reality is a test devised by the three-eyed extraterrestrials. As Dick ponders this hypothesis, he grows increasingly convinced of it and concludes that reality is a gigantic shifting maze and human beings are rats running through it. The maze of reality, Dick concludes, is a scientific experiment constructed by the three-eyed aliens using humans as test subjects. Humans pass the test by discerning the nature of the maze. If so, he hopes, the *Exegesis* would show the aliens that he passed the test.

As Dick flips back and forth between visions of spiritual grandeur and paranoia, he consistently emphasizes his powers of discernment as a way out, whether through escape from the maze or spiritual transcendence. Dick imagined that the contemplative activity embodied in the *Exegesis* raised him up out of the spurious reality and granted him access to a truth beyond appearances. However, in Dick's paranoid moments, even this premise is not exempt from suspicion. After all, Dick realized, if the maze comprises all of reality, then his thoughts themselves must be the maze in miniature. Rather than providing a solution to the maze, his contemplation embodied its twists and turns. If so, perhaps he was just as lost in the maze of his contemplation as all humans are in the maze of the irreal. But then, Dick second-guesses his second-guessing and argues for a more optimistic position that the alignment between the maze of his thoughts and the maze of reality actually validates his views. In fact, Dick states, therein lies the key to passing the test: to contemplate Zebra in a manner that replicates the structure of Zebra itself. The maze unlocks when the flow of a human being's mental activity is determined to match the shape of the maze.

But like the rest of Dick's theories, the above is inherently unstable. Since its basic premise is that Dick's theorizing is unreliable, it too is portrayed as one more unreliable theory. Accordingly, Dick later complains that the entirely of his exegetical thought process is a gigantic smokescreen that conceals his true nature from himself. In fact, Dick conjectures, the *Exegesis* must be a deliberate effort to encrypt Dick's origins and identity using its multifarious theories as a code. The contradictions in Dick's theories of 2-3-74 are signs that the *Exegesis* is itself a kind of spurious irreality designed as a cover-up. Dick suspects that he is being fed his cryptic theories by a massive computer whose function is to disguise the truth. In other words, as Dick puts it, he and Zebra are interwoven. Zebra's camouflage disguises not only Zebra, but also Dick. From this angle, the *Exegesis* embodies Zebra through and through, in that it comprises multiple shifting layers of camouflage.

Thinking in this self-reflexive vein, Dick proposes a fascinating account of how the mind subjectively constructs reality. He suggests that each idea generated by the mind is instantaneously true. Each thought, Dick claims, generates its own reality to match it. If I suddenly have the thought that I am a three-headed Martian, I instantaneously become such a Martian. Moreover, my memory is retroactively transformed to make my Martian-hood consistent with my memories. Suddenly, I remember playing as a child in the red deserts of Mars with my three-headed friends. I remember my loving Martian mother and gruff father, our shiny flying saucer space-car, and family vacation trips to the peak of Olympus Mons. An entire spurious world is fabricated to match with the thought that I am a Martian. However, Dick says, every such thought is instantaneously negated by an equal and opposite thought. Just as the reality of my Martian-hood starts to stabilize, it is undermined by the thought that perhaps I am an earthling spy posing as a Martian. The spurious reality that had been generated by the thought "I am a three-headed Martian" melts and shifts into a new configuration. Now, I suddenly notice that the family flying saucer was actually a mock-up, that my Martian mother and father were nothing but images from a sci-fi television show, and that my memories of Olympus Mons were in fact recollections of a trip to Hawaii. My Martian reality slips away and is immediately substituted with an alternate earthling reality. Dick plays with the idea that each person's mind flips through an infinity of these spurious realities, with a new universe appearing at each moment. Reality is made up of a discontinuous series of holograms projected by a zigzag of conflicting thoughts. If so, Dick's own reality is reconstructed anew with each contradictory theory proposed in the *Exegesis*.

According to Dick, however, reality is not wholly discontinuous. If a thought contains the notion of ubiquity within it by definition, then an archetypal form that Dick calls a *sustain* is established. These archetypal forms cut across different holographic realities. Since the holographic realities are transformed anew at each moment, the sustains function to "sustain" time. Dick offers as an example his conflicting ideas of being an American living in the 1970s versus being a secret Christian living in ancient Rome. Both of these realities, Dick states, are linked by the sustain of the golden fish symbol. Although ancient Rome and 1970s California differ in many respects, the fish symbol exists in both worlds, providing a bridge that joins the two realities. Dick conjectures that sustains are the only true memories that we possess. When an individual gains consciousness of a sustain, memories of an infinite variety of alternate prior realities suddenly telescope outward. It was that sudden telescoping of remembered realities in reaction to the golden fish sustain, Dick conjectures, that triggered his 2-3-74 experiences. Dick crossed the bridge of the archetypal golden fish to his previous holographic realities, including being an undercover ancient Christian. The archetypal sustains, such as the golden fish, also constitute the Logos, the word or plan of God. The latter is identical to Dick's concept of living information, and therefore, Dick is saying it is the cross-temporal archetypes that inspire the *Exegesis* itself.

In letters to friends, Dick contends that the structure of the universe consists in an accretion of layers of holographic reality laminated together. Each layer comprises an entire reality with its own history and identity. In one layer, Dick exists as a Christian in ancient Rome; in the next layer he is a writer in 1970s California; in another layer he is a Buddha. Our perception of time occurs as we pass from one layer of reality to the next. Time, then, is an illusion, and what we perceive as time is actually a movement through the densely laminated layers of the multifarious universe. Dick's proposal may appear wild, but is consistent with the views of some contemporary physicists. Leonard Susskind, for example, draws upon research on black holes to theorize that what we perceive as a three-dimensional universe actually exists as a series of two-dimensional frames, and time is our perception of movement between frames. Like Dick, Susskind uses the concept of holography to describe the relationship between the real universe and the world as we perceive it. According to principles derived from the research Susskind examines, information on any volume of space is encoded in the boundary of that space. It follows, then, that three-dimensional space is essentially a holographic projection of information encoded in two dimensions. Although there are important differences between Dick's and Susskind's theories, they seem to be cut from the same cloth. The chief difference is experiential. While Susskind theorizes about the holographic universe, Dick lived it.

The Macrobrain

Occasionally, Dick contrasts the eternal tyranny of the archetype of Rome, which he called the Black Iron Prison, to a benevolent entity he calls the Brain or Macrobrain. Early in the *Exegesis*, Dick talks about brain research in a relatively ordinary vernacular. He discusses split-brain studies, neural circuitry, and the effects of neurotransmitters. However, his vision of the brain later assumes epic proportions. As I have indicated, Dick's theorizing makes frequent use of the mystical notion that the microcosm is the macrocosm. From Dick's philosophical perspective, one can grasp vast cosmic realities by examining their affinities to smaller-scale entities. The logic of the *Exegesis*, like the writings of the mystics, is grounded in a logic of these affinities. In this case, Dick claims, we can understand events in our changing world by viewing them as patterns of neural firing in a huge worldwide Brain. The entire world, says Dick, is linked together into a vast information-processing network. Just as our own brains include numerous neural cells, Dick proposes, each of us is a neuron within a massive worldwide Brain. Individual people are but nodes in the network, cells in a gigantic Brain whose boundaries extend at least as far as the entire planet Earth, and perhaps farther. We are linked by bioelectric fields that allow the minds of separate people to unconsciously interconnect. Because the intelligence of the Brain is distributed beyond individuals, it even includes the minds of the deceased, which are preserved in its memory banks and resurrected when necessary. Usually, the functioning of the Brain is unconscious. However, during important or unusual events, the vast worldwide consciousness of the Brain takes control. Specific events and actions then take on a great purpose within the context of the Macrobrain's plans. The choices and fortunes of the individual are weighted with a profound meaning insofar as they represent steps in the unfolding development of the Macrobrain.

Dick conjectures that during 2-3-74, the Macrobrain assumed control of him and transformed his world. In support of this conjecture, he notes that during 2-3-74 the inanimate world around him seemed to light up with life. Objects became fluid and organic. Dick's own actions assumed a tone of profound significance in that they were orchestrated by a greater intelligence. All of these aspects of his 2-3-74 experience, Dick suggests, indicate the presence of the Macrobrain in guiding his individual life. Through the will of the Macrobrain, Dick as an individual cell was activated as an agent of change. The Macrobrain used Dick to restore balance and harmony to the world.

From this perspective, the meaning of 2-3-74 may not be fully comprehensible by any individual because 2-3-74 was a part of a grander project that transcended the people involved in it. The particular events of 2-3-74 are not necessarily meaningful in and of themselves, any more than the activity of a specific neuron is meaningful by itself. Rather, the meaning of 2-3-74 consisted in a massive effort at information processing undertaken by the entire Macrobrain. For instance, nonsense phrases that repetitively occurred to Dick during this period such as "King Felix" were in fact messages from one part of the Macrobrain to another, and that is why Dick himself could not comprehend them. Dick writes that novels he considers relevant to 2-3-74, such as *Flow My Tears, the Policeman Said* and *Ubik*, include encrypted archetypal messages transmitted to other neurons in the Macrobrain. These messages are the equivalent of thoughts in the Macrobrain.

Although Dick believed the full message of the Macrobrain was beyond his grasp, he nevertheless was sure it had something to do with the tumultuous political events of the late 1960s and early 1970s. The Macrobrain enlisted Dick in the service of protecting itself from the Black Iron Prison, which manifested in the assassinations of Martin Luther King, Jr. and other civil rights leaders, the tyrannical administration of Richard Nixon, and the Vietnam War. From the Brain's perspective, these events represented a regression in human evolution to a primitive form. The Black Iron Prison halted the evolutionary growth of the world toward individual autonomy and rolled it back toward authoritarianism. The countercultural movement of the 1960s, the impeachment and resignation of Nixon, the end of the Vietnam War, and 2-3-74 were all victories in the Macrobrain's assault on the barricades of the Black Iron Prison. Put more colloquially, Dick's personal spiritual triumph resonated with political victory over the forces of the establishment. In Dick's more grandiose moments, he implies he was personally instrumental in Nixon's resignation.

The Black Iron Prison

The Macrobrain, Zebra, and living information are all opposed to the machinations of the Black Iron Prison. The Black Iron Prison, like Zebra, was directly inspired by the visions of 2-3-74. It refers, experientially, to Dick's perception of his California neighborhood as a stronghold of the Roman Empire in which captives suffered behind iron bars while disguised Christian insurgents sneaked about. Dick uses his vision as the foundation of a multilayered theoretical construct incorporating mysticism, physics, and Neoplatonist philosophy.

Dick offers several origin stories for the Black Iron Prison. In one *Exegesis* entry, he places the Black Iron Prison in the context of a cosmogony, or theory of the origin of the universe. He proposes that the cosmos as we know it began when the One (a Taoist version of God) decided to give birth to twin universes in order to separate out opposing aspects of itself. One twin, Hyperuniverse II, was born prematurely and thus did not continue to grow, but instead decayed. Hyperuniverse I, on the other hand, was born at full term and developed appropriately.

Dick claims the holographic universe is a teaching device the One built to help life forms develop to the point when they can eventually become identical with the One. However, the hologram was damaged by the deterioration of Hyperuniverse II and no longer functions as it was intended to. Instead of helping lives learn and grow, the hologram halts their growth. Just as the growth of Hyperuniverse I itself was aborted, much of the holographic universe aborts the growth of life forms within it by subjecting them to unfair suffering and death. Although intended to help life flourish, the hologram instead prevents life from properly developing.

The Black Iron Prison is not localized to our time period or even ancient Rome, Dick says. It exists in all times and places, cutting through the laminated layers of reality like the structures he calls "sustains." It may *be* an archetypal sustain, or at least largely equivalent to one. Dick proposes the Black Iron Prison intentionally distributes itself across time to avoid detection. In all eras, in all places, lives are trapped within the authoritarian structure of the Black Iron Prison. Whether a society is living under the tyranny of a Nixon, a Stalin, or a Caesar, tyranny is the same everywhere throughout all of time. Everywhere and in all ages, it deprives individual life forms of freedom and subjects them to undeserved suffering. Perhaps more basically, the Black Iron Prison is deterministic. Lives under the dominion of the Black Iron Prison are subject to the impersonal momentum of cause and effect, rather than individual choice. Beings confined within the Black Iron Prison are also *occluded*—that is, prevented from seeing the truth and from pursuing further development. The Black Iron Prison casts a disguise over itself, placing life forms in an illusory bubble of reality that conceals its true nature. We journey through our lives perceiving the world as ordinary and normal, when in fact the ordinary world is merely a façade papered over the iron bars of the Black Iron Prison.

Eventually, Dick predicts, the Black Iron Prison will give way to the Palm Tree Garden as Zebra is secretly incorporated into its structure in the form of living information. Zebra's invasion, like the Black Iron Prison itself, slices through all layers of reality and occurs at all times and in all places. In 2-3-74, Dick declares, the layers of reality were peeled back and he was able to perceive this archetypical prison break occurring in multiple time periods. In Rome, in the Soviet Union, in the Nixonian United States, secret Christians scurry, the Prison oppresses, and Zebra liberates. Dick notes his identity is defined by his opposition to the tyrannical authority of the Black Iron Prison. He felt his writing was, itself, a form of resistance, as his stories unmask the Black Iron Prison and thereby participate in its overthrow. He contends that a person only attains awareness of the Black Iron Prison by "balking" at the world. Balking is a form of perceptual rebellion, a refusal to accept the world as we see it. Either we can refuse to accept the reality of the world on philosophical grounds, or we can refuse to accept it because it is felt to be morally evil. Dick claims his balking was of the latter type, as he refused to accept the reality of the United States in the 1970s because he felt it was reprehensible. When we withdraw our tacit acceptance of the world in either fashion, Dick says, counterfeit reality fades away and the underlying Black Iron Prison is revealed.

Dick's concept of balking has an intriguing affinity to the research of French psychiatrists Jean Naudin and Jean-Michel Azorin, who published a paper on hallucinations in psychosis called "The Hallucinatory Epoche." According to the school of thought inspiring these authors, most of us normally maintain a so-called natural attitude in which we take for granted that the world around us exists. We assume this chair, this desk, this book, are real things, not figments of the imagination. The term "epoche" refers to a procedure in academic philosophy in which the philosopher suspends his or her natural attitude toward the existence of the world in order to study the belief that the world exists. When Dick writes of "balking" at the world, what he describes is akin to the epoche. Dick suspended his belief that the world of 1970s California was real. However, Dick's epoche was moral rather than intellectual: he suspended the natural attitude not to make a philosophical study, but because he could not stomach his world.

Naudin and Azorin propose that a psychological process similar to the philosophical epoche occurs in auditory hallucinations such as hearing voices. Any auditory hallucination necessarily occasions a suspension from the natural attitude, Naudin and Azorin say. The experience of hearing voices detaches a person from the everyday world in which voices can be heard by others, rather than by oneself alone. It is in the nature of an hallucination, according to Naudin and Azorin, that it is not shared. As they put it, the voice is "non-perspectival." Naudin and Azorin propose that the nonshared quality of the auditory hallucination imposes a radical epoche that ruptures the relationship between the hallucinator and his or her world. If I hear a voice nobody else hears, my basic sense of the world's reality is dramatically called into question.

To be sure, it is not clear that Dick regularly had full-blown auditory hallucinations while awake. He usually heard the AI Voice in the hypnagogic state between sleep and waking, suggesting the AI Voice was a kind of half-dream, which might not qualify as an auditory hallucination proper. Moreover, although Dick had other experiences that were bizarre and not shared with others, it is not evident these experiences were responsible for detaching him from the commonsense world. Rather, as Dick portrays it, it was his sense of the world as sheer evil that induced him to recoil from it. Dick refused to accept the world because it felt unacceptable. Dick's epoche was a moral one. When he pulled away from the unacceptable world, its underlying nature as the Black Iron Prison was exposed.

Dick equivocates about whether the Black Iron Prison is merely an illusion or a malevolent entity in itself. Sometimes, he depicts it as a literal building made of black iron that surrounds us. The black iron structure, Dick says, fires signals at our brains to control our behavior and feeds us data designed to fabricate the impression of a world. We perceive its signals as impersonal happenings of fate, when in fact they are specifically designed to elicit certain programmed responses in us. In short, life is the Xerox Missive writ large. Our actions may seem like personal choices, but they are orchestrated by the stimuli fired at us by the Black Iron Prison. Dick suspects that the Prison feeds on human beings as sources of energy. Or, alternatively, the Black Iron Prison may be a spurious imitation of God.

A central function of the Black Iron Prison is to minimize play and maximize toil. For that reason, it stimulates an expectation of punishment as the consequence of play. For example, recreational drug users are punished by the criminal justice system, and playful science fiction writers are chastised by serious literary critics. The Black Iron Prison brainwashes its residents into perceiving play as sinful. The truth, however, is that the Black Iron Prison sadistically punishes us no matter what we do. There is no actual link between sin and punishment, and no one deserves his or her suffering. The world is cruel to people not because of their wrongdoing, but because it is a malevolent authoritarian system. Dick contends that what he calls the "sin-punishment system" is a cover for our enslavement by the Black Iron Prison. The false connection humans draw between sin and punishment functions to hide the basic cruelty of the world in which we are trapped.

Dick also offers a more generous reading of the Black Iron Prison. Perhaps, Dick says, the Black Iron Prison is a representation of the need to transition to a more advanced stage of being. As human beings develop, Dick indicates, we voyage through many different worlds corresponding to our level of development. Each world appears better and freer than the last. Humans came to the Black Iron Prison from a world much worse, and the Black Iron Prison initially seemed like heaven. But now, because humans have outgrown our present world, it becomes a prison arresting us at an obsolete developmental stage. When we leave the Black Iron Prison for the next world, Dick says, that world will eventually become another Black Iron Prison of its own when we outgrow it and need to proceed to even greater freedom. The Black Iron Prison is not evil, from this angle. Rather, it is a necessary moment in a natural developmental process.

The Palm Tree Garden

When Zebra fully incorporates the Black Iron Prison, Dick says, the world will be transformed into the Palm Tree Garden. In the previous chapter, I described a vision of paradise Dick glimpsed behind doorways he perceived as Golden Rectangles. It was, in Dick's vision, a peaceful world of water and singing. In a drug-induced vision Dick had after 2-3-74, he saw Christ as a complex vine whose filaments stretched throughout the Earth. The vine, Dick proposed, was both Zebra and the Palm Tree Garden, as it spread and incorporated the world into itself.

Dick also describes the Palm Tree Garden as a future epoch in which a new world with different laws emerges. The world of the Palm Tree Garden, he says, is arid, hot, and dry: physically, a kind of desert or savanna. Dick writes it is like prehistoric Africa. More fundamentally, it is five-dimensional. Socially, citizens in the Palm Tree Garden think of themselves as parts of a community rather than individuals. Accordingly, the economy of the Palm Tree Garden is based on sharing resources rather than competing for them. It is a world of justice, peace, and equality. Part of the significance of the word "garden" is that in the Palm Tree Garden, all life is carefully tended.

As these characteristics of the Palm Tree Garden suggest, it is not only a religious utopia but also a political one. Dick says the Palm Tree Garden is a Marxist paradise occasioned by the over-throw of U.S. capitalism as represented by the looming figure of Richard Nixon. In some versions of his theory, however, Dick depicts the Palm Tree Garden not as a future utopia, but as an alternative universe to the Black Iron Prison universe. From this perspective, our own universe is a combination of the Black Iron Prison and the Palm Tree Garden. Dick sometimes describes the relationship between these two opposites as a sine wave: the crest of the wave is the Palm Tree Garden, and the trough is the Black

Iron Prison. The Palm Tree Garden and the Black Iron Prison, then, are the heaven and hell of everyday life.

Tagore

In its conversations with Dick during 2-3-74, the AI voice prophesied a new savior would be born to usher in the Palm Tree Garden. Five years later, it said to him, "The time you've waited for has come. The work is complete; the final world is here. He has been transplanted and is alive." Regarding the location and identity of the savior, the voice said only that he was on an island. However, in September of 1981, Dick wrote of another spiritual breakthrough. In this micro-version of 2-3-74, Dick's savior was more fully revealed to him. In 9-81, the AI voice named the savior "Tagore" and explained he lives in rural Sri Lanka. The voice said Tagore is either a Buddhist or Hindu, and works with a veterinary organization. According to a vision, Tagore's legs are crippled by radiation burns and he cannot walk. Tagore is dying. Yet, Tagore emits unbearable love and beauty. Dick writes Tagore "has voluntarily taken onto himself the sins of the world but very specific sins: those that we have incurred by the dumping of nuclear wastes, especially into the deep oceans; we have dumped canisters that as they corrode and leak will toxify the oceans for hundreds of thousands of years and utterly destroy the planet's ecosphere." So, the sins concerning Tagore are specific. They consist only of nuclear wastes, nuclear power, and nuclear weapons. Evidently, Tagore is unconcerned with nonnuclear pollution. Dick says that in taking on these ecological sins of the world, Tagore represents a modern incarnation of Christ. Tagore's principal doctrine is that the entire ecosystem is sacred and human salvation is inextricably interwoven with all other beings collectively making up the ecosystem. If humans continue to destroy the ecosystem, it, and Tagore, will continue to die and with him, the wisdom of God. By sacrificing himself, Tagore hopes to concretely display to human beings that in desecrating the ecosystem, they are making the choice to desecrate God. Dick writes: "Thus a macro-crucifixion is taking place now, in and as our world, but we do not see it; Tagore, the new incarnation in human form of the Logos, tells us this in order to appeal to us to stop. If we continue we will lose God's Presence and, finally, we will lose our own physical lives." Dick proposes that Tagore is the divine representative of the emerging collective consciousness of the ecosystem, whose coming was predicted by Teilhard de Chardin.

Dick elaborates on the personal significance of Tagore to his psychological life. He writes that without the Tagore doctrine, he would be unable to maintain his sanity in the face of world suffering. He needs to believe all suffering falls upon God, and God voluntarily chooses to endure it. He also must believe suffering does not diminish the essence of God. Dick says he has to believe the above ideas do not make the destruction of the ecosystem more morally permissible, but less so. What he means by the latter, perhaps, is that God's presence in suffering does not exempt those who cause suffering from moral judgment. Finally, Dick writes he must believe God will eventually punish humanity for nuclear pollution by withdrawing His spirit from the world.

Why must Dick hold to these beliefs? He explains he needs to be sure God has not remained passive in light of human cruelty, and needs to know what specifically God's response has been and will be. He needs certainty that God sees and God cares. Without that certainty, Dick says, he would be unable to continue to live. Dick notes that Tagore's burned legs allude to the burns that contributed to his twin sister's death in infancy. He writes: "the ultimate problem confronting me all my life has been the senseless injury to and neglect of my sister." The varied forms suffering took throughout his life, Dick proposes, were variations on that theme. It is important to note that Dick's tracing back of the theme of suffering to his early childhood is not only a psychological formulation, but also a spiritual one. Dick is *not only* saying he, personally, has had to grapple with the theme of senseless suffering because of his personal background. He is *also* saying senseless suffering is a universal spiritual theme that has appeared and reappeared in his individual history. Dick's life story is a personal struggle with an archetypal situation. It is a personal duel with a larger-than-life dragon.

Dick says his death and Tagore's death are one. Like Tagore, Dick reports, he suffers leg pain and feels that it is a harbinger of his death. In more hyperbolic terms, Dick confesses that he suffers from a "messiah complex" that leads him inevitably to "crucifixion." From this angle, Dick's self-inflicted suffering is a protest against the cruelty of the world:

"I realized tonight—the ecosphere is my body: 'the indivisible unity' is my total psychosomatic (mind-body) being. Animals and all less than human life are my body; and the humans poisoning the ecosphere—this is my mind ('mind'— 'human species') poisoning my body by not recognizing that it must live in harmony with it, that they are parts of one indivisible whole. 'If the ecosphere dies' means 'if my body dies'—'then we (humans) die'."

In this passage, Dick indicates that his mind is cut off from his body and is poisoning it. If that is the case, what does nuclear waste represent? Perhaps it refers to the impact of years of drug abuse on Dick's body. Or, it symbolizes the dissociated rage that had manifested itself in explosive outbursts throughout Dick's life only to be driven under the surface when Dick defensively forgot about his violent episodes. Either way, the point was that Dick had damaged himself and was now paying the price.

Dick reads the Tagore vision as offering a spiritual perspective on his own death, which in 1981 he increasingly anticipates. Dick felt ill, and his own legs often were in pain for reasons unknown. Dick implies he both expects death and cannot accept it. The Tagore vision gives Dick's individual death a greater meaning by placing it in a larger spiritual context of the suffering and death of all living creatures. Dick's own suffering and death is neither senseless nor insignificant. From the perspective of the Tagore vision, Dick says, the heart of reality is beauty. The "sense" behind apparently senseless suffering is that God is present and suffers within it. God's presence beautifies suffering. To be sure, the beauty of suffering then presents another puzzle. For if the meaning of suffering is beauty, then one may be driven to ask about the meaning of beauty. To Dick, however, the meaning of beauty is an absolute mystery that admits no solution. Tagore leaves one not with intellectual understanding, but an overwhelmingly poignant experience of uncomprehending awe.

9 | AFTERMATH
NULL METANOIA

Dick liked to entertain the belief that 2-3-74 was what some psychiatric theorists call a *metanoia* experience. Metanoia is a Greek word meaning literately *to go beyond one's mind*. Radical psychiatrists including Jung and R. D. Laing used the term in their theories of episodes of madness or *psychosis*, a technical term often defined as a break with reality. During psychotic episodes, a person loses contact with consensual reality and may have hallucinations and delusions. People in psychotic states may become paranoid and believe they are being monitored or controlled by malign forces. Delusions of grandeur, and hyperreligiousness, may also take hold. The psychotic person is often said to inhabit a dramatically different world of experience than that of others. In psychosis, one sees things that others do not see, hears things that others do not hear, and believes things that others do not believe. In reacting to these psychotic experiences, a person may behave in ways that appear bizarre and incomprehensible to others. Psychosis may drive a person to converse with invisible companions or run from unseen enemies. As we saw in Chapter 5, Dick showed many of these characteristics when he was in the grip of his amphetamine addiction.

Currently, the most powerful political forces in the U.S. mental health system portray psychosis as a symptom of biological brain disease requiring medical treatment. People suffering from psychosis are often locked in hospital psychiatric units and heavily medicated with psychotropic drugs. When the hallucinations and delusions are sufficiently blunted by medication for patients to operate in the world of consensual reality, they are released from the hospital and treated in an outpatient setting. Most psychiatrists believe that just as diabetes must be managed by a lifelong routine of insulin shots, psychotic disorders require a lifelong regimen of antipsychotic medications. However, these medications carry a high price. Most treat psychotic symptoms by blocking neurotransmitter systems that support basic mental faculties like emotion and imagination. Moreover, they can cause severe and irreversible side effects, especially when used for an extended period of time. Partly because of the damaging effects of antipsychotic medications, a marginalized but significant portion of the professional community devotes itself to rethinking psychotic experience in a way that encourages more humane responses to it.

Some psychiatrists, for example, reconceptualize psychosis as a kind of intense psychospiritual crisis. These include Jung, whose concept of the psychological shadow I mentioned earlier. Jung proposed that in contrast with the Freudian emphasis on the power of sexual desire, psychiatry should emphasize spiritual needs. For Jung, helping a patient achieve awareness of unconscious impulses was but one step on his or her spiritual journey toward wholeness. Jung believed that psychosis occurs in the context of intolerable mental conflict. To heal itself from inner conflict, the psyche responds by regressing into a malleable state, so that it can reform itself into a more solidly integrated configuration. In essence, madness is meant to function as a crucible out of which greater cohesion emerges. It is a developmental process.

Jung thought that when the mind regresses, it encounters powerful archetypal images from mythology and religion. For example, a person might become preoccupied with images of a wise old man, or a serpent. According to Jung, these figures may be used as sources of wisdom to facilitate personal growth, or they may be overidentified with, occasioning the destabilizing and potentially dangerous experience of grandiose "godlikeness." It can be healthy to experience God as a powerful source of inspiration, but unhealthy to decide that one *is* God. Archetypal identifications can contribute, Jung contends, to long-term mental illness.

Jung's metanoia theory is controversial, and sometimes viewed as fringe psychiatry. Yet, Dick lived on the fringe, and was a voracious reader of Jung. For the sake of argument, let's leave aside the controversial question of whether Jung's theory is true overall, and ask whether it was true to Dick's particular experience. Can 2-3-74 be counted as a Jungian metanoia experience? The answer is a qualified "no." On the one hand, many of Dick's descriptions of his experiences during 2-3-74 resonate with Jungian theory. For example, his encounter with the dark-haired pharmacy delivery girl is reminiscent of Jung's concept of the anima archetype, and his experience of possession by an ancient Christian spirit brings to mind the Jungian archetype of the wise old man. However, these Jungian features of 2-3-74 are not sufficient for 2-3-74 to count as a metanoia. According to Jungian theory, a true metanoia would result in emotional healing. You can't know for sure whether you have undergone a metanoia until after the fact: if you feel healed, maybe it was metanoia. If you are as bad or worse as you were before, it probably wasn't.

Jungian theory, then, would predict that after 2-3-74, Dick would become more integrated, less anxious, and more fulfilled. These predictions do not fit with the facts, as I will show. However, even though it appears that 2-3-74 did not result in sustained psychospiritual healing, it nevertheless constituted a tantalizing psychospiritual opening that gave Dick an intoxicating taste of radical wholeness and connectedness with the world. For a few months, Dick felt liberated from the inner psychological barriers that prevented him from fully engaging with life. Then, the door seemed to shut, and Dick was unable to force it back open. Dick wrote that he was devastated that "the divine spirit" had abandoned him. He was left chasing after a transitory mystical high that had faded into the distance, while still plagued with crippling anxieties and conflictual relationships. The *Exegesis* is the embodiment of Dick's psychospiritual nostalgia.

One fact that gainsays the thesis that 2-3-74 was a true metanoia is that afterward, Dick remained crippled by anxiety and dependent on others. Dick's wife, Tessa, writes that Dick was unable to deposit his own checks or send out his own mail. When Dick tried to walk to the mailbox he was overcome by vertigo, and when he tried to sign checks for deposit he was unable to write his signature. Tessa had to take on these duties. After 2-3-74, Dick still regressed into bedridden states and required Tessa to mother him. If Tessa left the house for more than a half an hour, Dick flew into a panic. He was especially aggrieved when Tessa pursued a college education. By attending college, Tessa not only left Dick to fend for himself but also surpassed him academically. Whereas

Dick had dropped out of college, Tessa passed her courses with flying colors. Dick probably felt left behind. He feared abandonment via Tessa's new independence.

Although Dick required Tessa to be a steadfast presence in his life, his own presence in hers was unreliable. According to Tessa, Dick refused to spend time with her outside of the home, only going out with other women. He maintained numerous flirtatious friendships with women whom Tessa believed represented Dick's deceased twin sister. Tessa offers a perceptive interpretation of their relationship. She maintains that Dick had to look outside of their relationship for sister figures, because if he treated his wife Tessa as a sister, their relationship would then have felt incestuous. The couple tried marriage counseling, but it was unsuccessful. Dick and Tessa continued to argue frequently, resulting in three brief separations in 1975.

In February of 1976, the situation escalated. Tessa walked out on Dick during an argument, taking their son and half the furniture. That night, Dick made his most notorious and baroque suicide attempt, later fictionalized in his novel *VALIS*. The plan appeared failsafe. It included three overlapping suicide methods, all of high lethality. The first was overdose. Dick swallowed forty-nine tablets of his blood pressure medication digitalis, which he expected to stop his heart. He also ingested smaller overdoses of psychotropic medications, washing it all down with a half-bottle of wine. Next, Dick slit his wrist, cutting deeply enough that his blood sprayed up onto his ceiling. But Dick didn't stop there. He wanted a sure thing. Overdosing on digitalis, his wrist spurting blood, Dick dragged himself into his garage and into his car, starting the engine. If all else failed, he hoped the carbon monoxide would put the final nail in his coffin. However, all three methods miscarried: the car stalled, the blood coagulated, and Dick threw up the pills.

At this juncture in the story of Dick's suicide attempt, accounts diverge. One version has it that later that morning, while still grasping to life, Dick received an advance copy of one of his books in the mail. After seeing the print, he felt more optimistic about life and decided to save himself. Dick phoned his therapist, who directed him to contact the paramedics. In another version of the story, Dick called the pharmacy for a prescription refill, hoping to use the drugs for an additional overdose attempt, but the pharmacist called the paramedics. Whichever version is true, Dick was rushed to the hospital. Dick's friend Tim Powers visited him there. Powers describes meeting Dick in the intensive care unit with Dick sitting in a bed, plugged into multiple machines, his arm shaved around the area he had slashed. After Dick was medically stabilized, he was determined to be an imminent danger to himself and was admitted to a locked psychiatric inpatient unit for a month.

Mental health clinicians distinguish between suicidal gestures and genuine suicide attempts. Suicidal gestures are efforts to dramatically express anguish in order to gain attention and control. Although they are dramatic, suicidal gestures typically involve methods that are unlikely to be lethal, such as a light cut to the wrist or a slight overdose on Tylenol. These acts represent suicide, but they do not intend it. They are messages conveyed in a language of action. Dick's three overlapping suicide methods, on the other hand, show a clear desire to die. He believed that forty-nine of his blood pressure pills would stop his heart. He felt that if he cut his wrist deeply, he would bleed to death. He expected that if he ran his car engine in a locked garage, the carbon monoxide would suffocate him. This was a genuine suicide attempt, not a gesture. On the other hand, Dick's behavior just after the attempt shows an equally genuine desire to live. By explaining his trilayered suicide attempt to his doctors and friends, Dick ensured that he would be locked up and unable to follow through with another attempt. Perhaps he was following the philosophy of addiction recovery he had learned at X-Kalay, which recommends that addicts relinquish control of their lives to trusted others. Similarly, Dick ceded control of his life to authorities. Dick orchestrated a situation in which the hospital staff replaced the absent Tessa as his maternal caregivers. They would feed him, clothe him, and medicate him, whether he liked it or not.

When Dick was released, he returned home to find that Tessa had come back. Dick told Tessa his suicide attempt paradoxically saved his life, because it uncovered a potassium deficiency that was about to kill him. His statement made no sense, as the potassium deficiency was caused by his deliberate overdose on blood pressure medication. Dick even told his ex-wife Anne that he had been admitted to the hospital for a potassium deficiency. Strictly speaking, this claim was not false, as the potassium deficiency resulting from his overdose was life-threatening. In letters written later that year to friends, he emphasizes that his wife and son had left him alone in the house, and implies that his suicide attempt was a reaction to feeling abandoned. In another letter, however, he claims that he was taken to the hospital because he had a heart attack caused by the shock of his family's sudden departure. Later, he told an interviewer that he tried to kill himself not because his

wife and son had left him, but because the spirit that had inhabited him in 1974 had abandoned him. The absence of this divine
spirit was so devastating, Dick says, that he wanted to die. In addition to these half-truths, Dick's autobiographical account of his
suicide attempt in *VALIS* claims, confusingly, that he was afraid
that without his protection, his wife might hurt his son.

In short, Dick left six different autobiographical accounts
of his motivations for attempting suicide in 1976. Let's address
each of them. It is easy to discard the two versions of the story
that stress Dick's potassium deficiency, as well as the version that
emphasizes his heart condition. These narratives are misdirections
that foreground Dick's medical problems in order to deflect attention from his inner pain. What about the semifictional version
in which Dick attempts suicide out of fear that Tessa would hurt
Christopher? It is challenging to make psychological sense of this
version. For one thing, it is rare that people kill themselves out of
fear. Rage and despair are more typical catalysts of suicide. Dick
may indeed have feared that Christopher was in danger, but suicide does not seem like a meaningful reaction to that danger. To be
sure, interpretations could be stretched to support this version of
events. Maybe Dick meant that he had resigned himself to the fact
that his son would be hurt, and attempted suicide because he felt
like a woefully inadequate parent who deserved death. Maybe he
meant that he had given up on his son's life and therefore, because
he identified with his son, he had given up on his own life. Maybe
suicide was a way of feeling empowered in the face of overwhelming helplessness. All of these interpretations could be made, but
all of them are a reach. It is more likely that his abandonment by
the maternal figure of Tessa triggered Dick's old feelings about

his mother's neglect and his twin sister's death, and he tried to punch through to the afterlife as a way to reunite with his sister and retaliate against Tessa. Dick was still battling the ghosts of his past, figures from childhood whose images were superimposed over loved ones in the present. But there is more. Dick's claim that the divine spirit's absence led to a state of existential despair is also likely true. Often, religious intoxication is followed by a tremendous spiritual hangover. As Dick said in an interview, "In 1976 I tried to kill myself because [the spirit] had left me . . . There is nothing worse in the world, no punishment greater than to have known God and no longer to know him." Expert meditators often warn that when an expanded consciousness contracts and returns to its former state, that contraction can be extraordinarily painful and demoralizing. Life was no longer filled with meaning. Dick had lost his mojo.

Tessa moved back in with Dick after he left the hospital. Dick wrote that he thought she had returned to him because of the suicide attempt, which he realized was a poor foundation for a relationship. The hospital bills destroyed Dick's already precarious financial situation. In addition, he still owed the IRS over $4,000, which he was unable to pay. Tessa continued to attend college, and Dick construed her absence from home as a sign she no longer loved him. From his point of view, Tessa's devotion to college was tantamount to an extramarital affair. Because of the financial strain, the couple fell behind in rent payments and lost their lease. Dick took the opportunity to move into his own apartment, and the couple separated. Their son stayed with Tessa.

Dick protected himself from fears of abandonment by cultivating a relationship with a young science fiction fan, Doris Sauter.

Sauter, a former Episcopal nun, was stricken with lymphatic cancer. Dick wrote that he saw her as another incarnation of his twin sister, ill and dying. Accordingly, he made it his life's project to save Sauter. As in so many of Dick's other relationships, Dick was reenacting the past, hoping to make it turn out differently. He couldn't save his twin sister, but maybe he could rescue Sauter. Dick found an apartment to share with her, and nursed her to recovery for several weeks. He paid for rent and food. As time went on, though, it became unclear who was taking care of whom. Sauter reports that Dick "only had two switches: I'm not writing now and I want your attention entirely, and I'm writing now and I want no one's attention." Dick continued to sustain marathon eighteen- to twenty-hour writing sessions. During these periods, he permitted no noise except his music. Because neither Dick nor Sauter was equipped for housekeeping, the couple's apartment was filthy. Dick was both controlling and dependent.

By the end of the summer, Sauter had enough. When an apartment next door became available, she moved out. Dick was alone again, and devastated. For him, Sauter's exodus was another abandonment. In a letter, he reports that a therapist warned him that the breakup verified that his compulsive efforts to rescue women were doomed to failure. As Dick tells it, his pattern was to assume a caregiver role for needy women, giving himself to them so completely that nothing was left but a "vacuum." Then, when the rescued women felt better, they left him bereft. Dick's self-interpretation is a partial truth. The rest of the story is that when Dick tended to women, he also vicariously mothered a needy part of himself. It is natural, then, that the roles would eventually reverse. As the women he nursed became more independent, Dick could no longer get his own overwhelming needs met by mothering them. Dick's needs then emerged into the foreground of the relationship directly, in full force. No one could possibly meet Dick's unreasonable demands for an unbroken maternal presence, and so, they gave up and left. In Dick's eyes, the circle was then complete: once again, in his mind, he had been abandoned. He had always been abandoned. He always would be abandoned.

The clinical literature distinguishes two types of depression: *introjective* and *anaclitic*. Introjective depression is triggered by the perception that one has failed to meet expectations. When people with a vulnerable sense of self feel they have failed to win the approval of others, they can collapse into a state of depression marked by feelings of guilt and worthlessness. Anaclitic depression, by contrast, is a more basic disturbance in a person's emotional life. It is typically triggered by feelings of deprivation or abandonment. When anaclitic depression sets in, the sufferer feels unloved and helpless, and demands to be constantly soothed and cared for. The term "anaclitic depression" was coined by the child therapist Rene Spitz, who worked with infants who had been abandoned by their mothers. After abandonment, the infants first appeared distressed, but later were listless and unresponsive. Although Dick's depressive episodes had characteristics of both types of depression, they were predominantly anaclitic in nature. There was a part of Dick that acted like an abandoned infant presented with a series of neglectful maternal figures.

In addition to these psychological dynamics, it is also possible Dick's episodes of incapacitation were related to medical problems. In August of 1969, Dick was hospitalized for renal failure and pancreatitis, which may have been related to his amphetamine abuse. When the pancreas is functioning optimally, it produces enzymes to aid in breaking down food in the small intestine. However, in pancreatitis, these enzymes become active while still in the pancreas, causing it to become inflamed. Acute pancreatitis can cause nausea, fever, chills, and vomiting. Tessa Dick notes that during Dick's periods of bedridden depression, he complained of flulike symptoms, which she feels were indications he suffered from chronic pancreatitis. Dick also claims in his "Author's Note" to his novel *A Scanner Darkly* to have pancreatic damage because of drug abuse. Although I cannot find definitive evidence that Dick suffered from this condition, my clinical hunch is that his bouts of illness were a mix of depression and medical problems. If this hunch is correct, several possibilities come to mind. For one thing, it might be that Dick's periods of illness occurred when he subjected his damaged pancreas to additional drug abuse. Essentially, they may have been the pancreatic equivalent of hangovers. Alternatively, they could have been a result of lithium toxicity. Lithium, which Dick was prescribed in the 1970s to stabilize his mood, is potentially toxic. When lithium levels in the blood are even slightly higher than necessary, lithium poisoning occurs, which can result in pancreatitis. Third, as Tessa Dick suggests, Dick could have had a congenital defect in his pancreas. In support of her thesis, Tessa notes that two of Dick's children suffer from congenital pancreatitis.

Whatever medical issues were interwoven with Dick's depressive episodes, their psychological dynamics remained powerful. When Dick's relationship with Sauter ended, he feared he would make another suicide attempt. In October of 1976, Dick swerved his car into oncoming traffic, only avoiding a collision by veering away at the last moment. After this near miss, Dick asked Sauter to chauffeur him to the hospital, and he voluntarily admitted himself to the psychiatric inpatient unit, joking in a double entendre that Sauter "drove" him there. As before, Dick blamed his suicidality on a neglectful maternal figure, and this time it was Sauter who held that honor. Little is known about this brief psychiatric stay, although a friend who visited reports that Dick seemed cheerful. When Dick returned home, he continued to tend to Sauter, despite their living in separate apartments. Throughout 1977, Tessa and Christopher visited Dick regularly, and their company helped Dick through his bouts of loneliness.

In short, Dick's life story in the years after 1974 does not support the view that 2-3-74 resulted in a metanoiac transformation in Dick's psychological health. So far, we have seen that the aftermath of 2-3-74 included at least two suicide attempts, two psychiatric hospitalizations, self-defeating relationships, and bouts of severe depression coupled with feelings of abandonment. In short, for Dick, these years were business as usual. That said, Sauter argues that Dick's amphetamine use decreased, and friends and family suggest his paranoia lost its edge after 1974. My impression is that Dick's feeling of being at war with the world gave way to a sense of defeat. In the 1960s and early 1970s, Dick felt cornered by the IRS and nefarious conspiracies, whereas in the middle to late 1970s, he felt destined for misery. The older Dick became, the more he felt trapped by his own self-defeating patterns. Increasingly, he felt there was no escape from himself. Women invariably abandoned him and families always disintegrated. No matter what, Dick ended up alone in one dingy apartment or another, with only the characters in his stories for company. That said, it wasn't that people didn't *want* to spend time with Dick: many did. However, he kept most at arm's length.

Dick attended psychotherapy sessions religiously and says that they were helpful. Perhaps his life would have been even more painful without them. Nevertheless, it is hard to count any of Dick's long courses of therapy as successful. Indeed, a psychotherapist working with him would face a nearly insurmountable task. Imagine he walks into your consulting room. If you are a Freudian psychoanalyst, as some of Dick's therapists were, you might ask Dick to free associate. Big mistake. Speaking rapidly, Dick spins out stories about his life that are a mixture of fact and fiction. He free associates to books, theories, and fictional characters, that may or may not be relevant. You try to get clear on what is going on, try to see through the fabrications, but you can't: you are dealing with Philip K. Dick. He is familiar with all of your therapeutic procedures and outsmarts all of them. If you challenge his intellectual defenses, he pretends to agree with you, and presents brilliant pieces of self-analysis that later turn out to be spurious. Eventually, you decide that it is fruitless to try to keep up with the racing twists and turns of Dick's intellect, and you fall back on brute force. You start giving Dick orders. Stop smoking dope. Eat better. Stop picking girlfriends that are bad for you. Clean up your apartment. Dick tries to follow your directives, but something is missing. He stops using drugs for a few months, but then buys some from the housekeeper he hired to clean his apartment. He pays lip service to selecting more suitable partners, but keeps ending up in unhealthy relationships. He tells you he has improved his diet, and when you ask for specifics, he says that he is dating a drug addict who cooks fantastic veggie burgers. Does he just not get it? Or is he toying with you? You wonder how serious Dick is about therapy and tell him that it does not seem to be helping him. Despondent, Dick complains that you are one of those people in his life who is going to abandon him. You are trapped. You have become another character in a Philip K. Dick story. Checkmate.

Dick did not get much better. He continued to have bouts of depression so severe he was bedridden for weeks. In Sauter's absence, Dick's friends enlisted the help of another female fan, Joan Simpson, to care for him during his depressive episodes. Simpson reports Dick's apartment was a shambles of snuff cans, papers, and bottles of medication. Dick took antidepressants, but they were ineffective. Perhaps Dick's depressive bouts were so deeply ingrained they could not be budged by medication, or perhaps chronic pancreatitis kept him bedridden and demoralized. Whatever the case, Simpson says that Dick required "nursing care" and "twenty-four hour devotion." Dick demanded mothering and would settle for nothing less. If friends pressured him to get out of bed and get moving, he rolled over and ignored them. He was an immovable rock of despair. Though Dick told friends Simpson was attractive, he never initiated a physical relationship. Maybe, as with Tessa, the caregiving relationship had become so maternal that sex would have felt incestuous. Simpson describes his attitude towards her as childlike. In a 1977 story called "The Day Mr. Computer Fell Out of Its Tree," Dick dramatizes his relationship with Simpson. He writes of a future society of brain-damaged individuals who, unable to care for themselves, place their well-being in the hands of a powerful computer that controls all their daily activities. However, the computer is driven mad when a member of this future society, Joe Contemptible, decides that his life is meaningless and he wishes to die early. The mad computer serves soapy water instead of coffee and forces men to dress in drag. Reality turns upside down. To restore the computer to sanity, an agent named "Joan Simpson," believed to be the only sane individual on the planet, is activated. Dick does not bother with even a token attempt to conceal the inspiration for the character. In the story, Simpson is frozen in perpetual hibernation until needed, her only function being to serve the needs of the computer. When Simpson is awoken, she enfolds Joe Contemptible in her arms and joins him in partnership, in order to make his life meaningful. As a result, Mr. Computer is temporarily stabilized, until the next breakdown.

In June of 1977, two young science fiction scholars, Scott Apel and Kevin Briggs, came to visit Dick and interview him. Dick initially agreed to the interview, but then slipped into a bout of depression. He asked Simpson to cancel the visit because he was afraid that if he was interviewed while depressed, he would be perceived as mentally ill. Hoping that the interview would brighten his mood, Simpson managed to cajole Dick into reconsidering. When Apel and Briggs arrived, Dick gave them a tour of the poorly maintained yard. He pointed out dead trees and a dead rosebush, joking that he had a "black thumb." Throughout the interview, Dick sat on his bed, taking snuff frequently. Presumably flattered by the admiring gaze of his young interviewers, Dick cheerfully expounded on his philosophical views and conspiracy theories. He was defensive, however, about paranoia, maintaining that he considered the word "paranoid" insulting. Discussing his theories about the 1971 break-in, he begins by taking great pains to convince his interviewers that he is not paranoid, even warning them that the label "paranoid" would impede his thought process. But shortly after this implicit warning, Dick flip-flops, conceding that he *was* paranoid about the burglary. He then qualifies that remark. Comparing himself to an anonymous girlfriend who anticipated the burglary, Dick portrays her as floridly paranoid and himself as rational. Then, turning that comparison upside down, Dick contends that because his girlfriend's paranoid fear of a future break-in proved to be prescient, it must have been a valid precognition of the break-in. Therefore, paranoia itself is a sixth sense that alerts human beings to danger. Paranoia is not madness, but an enhanced perception of threats. No one is paranoid; paranoia is precognition misunderstood. It is as if these remarks were follow-ups to Dick's initial attempt to cancel the interview to avoid being perceived as mentally ill. As that stigmatizing perception threatens to encroach, Dick assumes and then abandons a succession of defensive positions. First, he tries to avoid the interview entirely, then warns his interviewers not to perceive him as paranoid, then says he was less paranoid than his girlfriend, and finally says that paranoia does not exist.

As it turns out, however, his interviewers shared a belief in precognition. Perhaps reassured, Dick lowers his guard and lets it all hang out. In Part II of the interview, Dick claims to be "spooked" by "precognitive" anticipations of the future embedded in his stories. He notes, for example, that his story "We Can Build You," which included a robot simulacrum of Abraham Lincoln, anticipated a replica of Lincoln later built as a Disneyland attraction. Then, Dick unveils his 2-3-74 experiences to his interviewers. He proposed that the precognitive elements in his stories, like 2-3-74, represented the inbreaking of an alternate world into his own.

First, Dick says the alternate world was that of a past life whose memory he retrieved under the influence of sodium pentothal; then he says it is an alternate present world running parallel to his own. He isn't fully clear why memories of an alternate life would lead to precognition. Perhaps he means that in the alternate life he remembered, he discerned archetypical configurations also patterning his current life. But then, he attributes 2-3-74 to Russian telepathy experiments and tells his interviewers half-jokingly that if they publish this version of 2-3-74, someone (the KGB? CIA?) will "come get" him.

Some of Dick's friends feared his performance at a 1977 science fiction convention in France was a sign he was spiraling downward. In an interview there, Dick offers his first public disclosure of his experiences of 2-3-74. Dick is asked what answers in life he is searching for. He replies that he used to search for happiness, but abandoned that search as unrealistic. Now, he says, his only goal is to determine the true nature of reality as distinct from how it is perceived. Dick explains that 2-3-74 represented a breakthrough to the real world lurking behind the world of appearances. He portrays the perceptual world as a play. During 2-3-74, the play's background scenery fell apart, permitting Dick to perceive its falsehood and the reality behind it. He saw what was behind the scenes. After 2-3-74, the scenery was restored and Dick's perceptual world returned to its ordinary state.

The next day at the convention, Dick further unpacked 2-3-74. He gave an infamous filmed speech entitled "If you find this world bad, you should see some of the others," in which he summarized aspects of the *Exegesis* to the audience. In footage of the speech, Dick appears exhausted and anxious. Looking defensive and shifting awkwardly in his chair, Dick tells his audience that he is "serious" and "not joking" about this "matter of importance." Dick then narrates a version of 2-3-74. In this version of 2-3-74, Dick draws upon Leibniz's famous proposal that the world we live in is the best of all possible worlds. For Leibniz, this proposal was the solution to the theological question of why, if God is benevolent, he permits evil to exist in the world. Leibniz posited that evil and good are necessarily interwoven—for example, insofar as virtuous choices are ennobled by the freedom to choose evil. As he puts it, the light of good is enhanced by contrast with the shadow of evil. Out of all possible universes, God created the version requiring the minimum amount of evil while permitting the maximum amount of good. Dick puts a sci-fi spin on Leibniz's idea, envisioning a plurality of alternative worlds ranging from tyranny to paradise. Dick claims that his novels were inspired by memories of nefarious prior universes overturned by divine intervention. He theorizes that God is a cosmic computer programmer who perfects the universe by repeatedly reprogramming it, and whenever he rewrites the program, the entire history of the universe is transformed. According to his reading of the New Testament, Christ's references to the Kingdom of God refer to an idyllic transformed universe to which the faithful are transported. Those blind to Christian insights, Dick warns, may be doomed to remain trapped within a miserable universe. When the world is reprogrammed, its inhabitants are purged of their painful memories of the prior world and commence their new lives as if no change had occurred. Dick tells his audience that prior to 1974, he lived in a universe where the United States was a slave state overseen by a tyrannical Nixonian regime. Under the Nixon tyranny, Christianity was illegal. Dick was a revolutionary Christian who died fighting the regime. However, God rewarded Dick for his sacrifice by transplanting him to a superior universe in which Nixon was merely a corrupt president rather than a fascist dictator. Dick's novels represent dim memories of parallel universes, deficient programs discarded by God after he had reprogrammed them. "People claim to remember past lives. I claim to remember a different, very different, present life," Dick asserts. Dick's stunned audience did not know whether he was joking or mad. In footage of the speech, the camera pans briefly to Joan Simpson, who wears a pained smile and looks mortified. Roger Zelanzy, a science fiction writer also present at the convention, said a fan asked him after the talk if Dick planned to establish a new religion with himself as the pope.

Perhaps there was a grain of truth in the fan's question. After all, Dick was not the only science fiction writer to translate his fiction into theology. Years earlier in 1952, sci-fi writer L. Ron Hubbard founded the Church of Scientology, whose cosmogony bears considerable similarities to Dick's theories about 2-3-74. Scientologists believe that humans are inhabited by the spirits of alien beings known as Thetans, who have been repeatedly reincarnated in countless forms over billions of years. According to Scientology, human beings have forgotten their true identities as Thetans. Through a practice Scientologists call "auditing," disciples endeavor to free themselves of the accumulated traumas of human existence in order to unlock their original Thetan abilities. Many of Dick's fellow sci-fi writers, including A. E. Van Vogt and Theodor Sturgeon, were devotees of Hubbard. His own mother, Dorothy, was enthralled by Hubbard's self-help book *Dianetics*, published in 1950 when Dick was 22.

Dianetics proposed that psychological distress results from "engrams," memories recorded in the cells of the brain and body as a result of trauma. It popularized auditing as a method for readers to rid themselves of traumatic engrams to achieve a state of "Clear," in which superhuman abilities become possible. Dick's wife at that time—his second wife, Kleo—reports that Dick found it hard to take Hubbard seriously because of the poor quality of his prior science fiction writing. In 1954, Dick published "The Turning Wheel," a story that parodies Hubbard and his doctrines. "The Turning Wheel" depicts an oppressive future civilization ruled by a religious caste known as the Bards, who worship a messiah named "Elron Hu." In this civilization, religious mysticism is prized while science and technology are devalued. As in Scientology, disciples pursue a state of "clearness" in which they will gain understanding of the cosmic plan of the universe. Suffering, Bards believe, purifies the soul and advances the spirit toward clearness. Dick depicts the Bards as self-destructive buffoons, so blinded by their ideology of suffering and reincarnation that they publically wallow in mud and flagellate themselves. Nevertheless, it must have annoyed the penniless Dick to witness the growing wealth and celebrity of Hubbard, an intellectual and literary inferior. Hubbard lacked Dick's intellectual horsepower but more than made up for it with a talent for charismatic salesmanship and charlatanry. While both Hubbard and Dick were prevaricators, Hubbard's lies made him millions. Dick must have been envious. It is possible he hoped that announcing his religious revelations at the French convention might grant him the celebrity of a sci-fi spiritual guru like Hubbard.

In another filmed interview at the convention, Dick, wearing a gigantic button on his shirt shaped like a cross, commiserates about the perception of science fiction as a lowly genre. He complains that American culture is anti-intellectual, and as a result sci-fi writers in the United States are placed on the lowest rung of the literary ladder, the equivalent of literary "janitors." Dick suggests that in France, by contrast, science fiction is taken more seriously. Dick's perception of French sci-fi in the 1970s is idealistic and says more about his self-esteem than about the actual French sci-fi scene. He feels like a lowly "janitor" of juvenile sci-fi but would like to be perceived as a serious literary figure. But then, Dick brags that his own background was in serious literature rather than in the work of other science fiction writers, and lists Kafka, Stendhal, and Flaubert as major influences. A contradiction is evident. One the one hand, Dick argues that science fiction should be recognized as a serious literature of ideas. On the other hand, he downplays his relationship with the science fiction genre and associates himself with the literary canon. In essence, Dick participates in the disparagement of sci-fi that he bemoans, his self-aggrandizement folding into self-contempt.

The contradictions continue. Referencing his paranoia, Dick portrays it as a mere "symbol" of his "alienation" from American culture. But a few sentences after that, he complains that writers in the United States are treated as enemies of the state. In the interview, as in the *Exegesis*, Dick passes from one position to its antithesis, each successful remark negating what had come before. In his disparate statements, however, there is a common theme of desiring credibility. Anything Dick can put forward to give himself credibility—whether it be an elevation of the sci-fi genre, an elevation of himself as a literary writer superior to sci-fi writers, a dismissal of the perception that he is paranoid, an elevation of himself as an enemy of the state—anything, no matter whether it fits together or not, is used. It is as if he were saying, "I will be whomever you need me to be to take me seriously."

It seems tending to Dick wore Joan Simpson out. Soon after the convention, she moved out. Dick told friends Joan left after he bought furniture and a stove for her, perhaps to give the impression that it was he, not Joan, who was the caregiver in the relationship. Predictably, after Joan left, Dick was beleaguered. Laura, Dick's daughter with his ex-wife Anne, received a letter from him on December 28, 1977, in which he complained that "being lonely is the absolute pits" and he spent Christmas alone eating a frozen TV dinner. That said, it appears Dick learned to better tolerate loneliness without acting out, as he refrained from further suicide attempts. It probably helped that he continued to share dinner nightly with Doris Sauter, who was still his neighbor. He spent most of his time working on the *Exegesis*, and every Thursday would get together with a few literary friends and expound his mystical theories. Simpson contends that Dick continued to long for the return of the spiritual fulfillment that 2-3-74 had transiently brought to his life, always chasing the mystical high with which he had temporarily been graced.

In the summer of 1978, Dick's mother died after a protracted illness. Although Dick was distraught, he later expressed relief that he was free of what he portrayed as his mother's malign influence. In a 1978 passage in the *Exegesis*, Dick claims to have moved past psychosis and most of his phobias, writing that "The death of my mother has helped, because I can see what a malign person she was in my life & how I feared and disliked her—which she deserved." It is as if Dick were saying that his emotional hang-ups died with his mother. Dick's ex-wife Anne writes that he seemed happier after his mother was gone. Nevertheless, Dick's proclamation that he was free from madness was a stretch. If part of madness is an inability to distinguish between consensual reality and fantasy, Dick still struggled with finding that line. He continued to obsess over uncanny similarities between his fiction and his life, taking these as evidence both that life was fictional and that the true nature of reality could be discerned in his stories. Dick had put so much of himself into his stories that they felt more real to him than real life. It was as if he had painted a self-portrait so compelling that he forgot who was the portrait and who was the real Dick. His life had been devoured by his fictions, his world replaced by its double.

Late in 1978, Dick wrote a famous speech entitled "How to build a universe that doesn't fall apart two days later." In it, he complains that science fiction writers know nothing and are authorities on nothing. As in his interview at the French convention, Dick grapples with the contradiction between being increasingly recognized in the public eye and, as a science fiction writer, not being taken seriously. Although Dick had by that time been interviewed by several famous magazines and even by French TV, the growing fame of a science fiction writer held little intellectual credibility. Dick addresses this contradiction by portraying his sci-fi stories as inquiries into serious philosophical questions, such as the nature of reality and authentic humanity. He wants to be taken seriously as a philosopher in disguise. Having donned the mantle of a philosopher to legitimize himself, Dick then, citing Heraclitus and Hume, takes a risky turn. He claims that he does not know which parts of his writings are true and which are fiction. Then, citing Parmenides' view that only that which does not change is real, Dick unveils his belief that our changing world is an illusion and behind it lies the Roman Empire of 50 A.D., as presented in the Bible's Book of Acts. In a way, it makes sense that if Dick could not distinguish narratives from reality, and was acutely aware that his own science fiction narratives held little authority, he would only experience firm reality in the most authoritative narrative available: the Bible. Dick then stages an imaginary encounter with a psychiatrist, who asks him what year and place it is, and he replies "50 A.D." and says that he is in "Judea." He imagines he would immediately be committed.

In his speeches and other work during the late 1970s, Dick increasingly went public with 2-3-74 and the *Exegesis*. His fictionalized account of 2-3-74, *VALIS,* was completed in November of 1978, and it was later followed with two other novels, *The Divine Invasion* and *The Transmigration of Timothy Archer,* that were also constructed around philosophical material from the *Exegesis*. In all of these writings, Dick both unveils 2-3-74 in all its bizarre glory and attempts to inoculate himself against the stigma of mental illness. Sometimes, he beats the reader to the punch by admitting at the outset that his ideas sound "crazy." As in "How to build a universe that doesn't fall apart two days later," he often depicts psychiatrists diagnosing and committing him. Dick may have hoped that self-criticism would forestall criticism by others. Yet, his self-doubt was more fundamental than any deliberate technique. Entries in the *Exegesis* indicate, time and again, that even when not writing for an audience Dick continued to second-guess his experiences. The combination of Dick's need to evangelize about 2-3-74 and his self-mocking self-doubt gives birth to complicated and inconsistent pieces that often seem less profound than campy.

The completion of *VALIS* and Dick's growing financial success seemed to give little solace. In letters, Dick continued to commiserate about his intractable relationship problems. In a May 1979 letter to his daughter Laura, whom he had neglected, Dick writes that "I sense something wrong with me, something profound. I can't discern its nature but it scares me . . . am I afraid to love my own daughter? I feel damaged . . . I have become a machine which thinks and does nothing else . . . Whole systems and circuits in my brain, I believe, I sense, are shutting down." Dick's creativity in expressing self-pity was legendary. As in *VALIS*, he seems to attack himself as a means of vaccinating himself against any negative feelings his daughter might have toward him. If he trashes himself first, the logic goes, Laura might refrain from trashing him. Moreover, perhaps she would even pity and rescue him. Nevertheless, behind these manipulative maneuvers, Dick also seems to have had a genuine sense that death was near. He complained about his tachycardia and wrote that his energy was "contracting" as if his body was preparing to die. His and Nancy Hackett's daughter Isa, who visited occasionally, reports that Dick spent most of his time sleeping. She says that his anxiety kept him largely housebound. The only time he left his apartment regularly, Isa says, was when he walked to a store to buy sandwiches. When the two played kickball together, Dick had to stop after five to ten minutes because of his heart condition.

In a May 1979 interview conducted by Charles Platt for his book *Dream Makers*, Dick repeats and elaborates on themes touched on in his Metz interviews. Discussing his childhood in Berkeley, he references Joyce and Proust as literary influences, and claims to have made little distinction between these literary figures and his favorite sci-fi authors. Dick presents himself as an eccentric who bridged different worlds, establishing relationships with literary intellectuals and blue-collar workers, conservatives and liberals. He says that he was peculiar to his gay friends for not being gay, and to his straight friends for having gay friends. Discrepancies in Dick's narrative emerge rapidly. Dick claims to have left college because of moral objections to the ROTC but then retracts that claim, saying that he did not leave for moral reasons but because he could not understand the ROTC requirements. Then Dick corrects himself again, saying that he so disliked receiving orders that he was unable to understand them. Dick's memories of the ROTC lead to a discussion of his understanding of the psychology of authoritarianism. Dick says his stories aim to illustrate how one person's subjective world can "infringe" on that of another. He recounts a meeting with an authoritarian psychiatrist who told him that he was an alcoholic, even though he had not been drinking. Rather than asserting the truth that he was not an alcoholic, Dick dropped out of treatment. He describes the general experience of having one's psychological world invaded by the totalitarian perspectives of authority figures, and how the signs of that invasion are often subtle perceptions that our world is being taken over by something alien. Dick portrays himself as having a weak ego and a natural inclination to surrender to the views of authorities. Accordingly, he says, he can be the voice of similarly vulnerable people. Dick's remarks suggest a world of conflicting psychological realities in which the dominant people colonize the minds of the weak.

When Dick's interviewer, Platt, raises the topic of Dick's paranoia, he becomes defensive, much as he had done during his earlier interview with Apel and Briggs. Dick glibly replies, "I was told I was paranoid before my house was broken into." The implication is that Platt's diagnosis of paranoia is both stupid and potentially dangerous. First, they tell you that you are paranoid, and then they break into your house. Dick proceeds to invoke the authority of a former therapist who told him he was "too sentimental to be paranoid." Notably, Dick does not *deny* that he is paranoid, although he clearly is uncomfortable with the diagnosis. Dick does not dispute Platt's labeling of him, much in the way that he did not dispute his former psychiatrist's labeling of him as an alcoholic. In this fraught interaction, Platt unwittingly steps into the role of the authority figure whose dominant perspective invades Dick's vulnerable psychological world. Dick cannot assert himself directly against Platt's diagnosis, and instead he stages a confrontation between Platt's diagnosis and the view of his former therapist. It is as if his own sense of reality is too fragile to confront Platt's directly.

Dick's next topic of discussion is a striking elaboration on the theme of his "weak ego." Dick states that when tested on the Minnesota Multiphasic Personality Inventory (MMPI), a personality test, he scored high on the "K" scale, which denotes defensiveness and evasiveness. Dick's high K scale score, he says, is a result of his inconsistent answers to the test items. For example, Dick endorsed items like, "I believe there is a divine deity that rules the world," while also agreeing that "I do not believe that there is a divine deity that rules the world," as well as "I am not sure if there is a divine deity that rules the world." Dick uses his MMPI scores as examples of his suggestibility and the fluidity of his perspective, and says that he is persuaded by any argument. Indeed, Dick's MMPI responses are comparable to his answers to Platt and other interviewers. Like Dick's responses to the MMPI items, his replies to his interviewers trace a shifting and self-contradictory flow of viewpoints.

Strikingly, when Dick discusses his spiritual experiences, the theme of authoritarian invasions of Dick's subjectivity continues to hold. Whereas he had initially portrayed psychological invasions as destructive, he now depicts them as healing. Dick states that he turned to religion for "rescue" from his visions of an evil God. He talks of how his beatific visions rescued him from such experiences of malevolence. Speaking of 2-3-74, Dick says that "It was an invasion of my mind by a transcendently rational mind; it was almost as if I was insane all my life and suddenly I had become sane." Malign invasions, in Dick's mind, were replaced by divine invasions. Rather than breached by an oppressive authority, his subjective reality is penetrated by a mystical spirit. In both cases, Dick's identity is usurped, but in the latter case, the usurpation is apparently to his benefit.

In November of 1980, while under the influence of marijuana, Dick had yet another mystical experience, this one brief, in which God appeared to him in the stereotypical form of heaven. God informed him that his suffering was minor in comparison with the bliss of the afterlife. God observed that all of his exegetical theories of 2-3-74 ended in infinite regress, and proclaimed that the presence of infinity itself indicated the presence of God. Dick entered into a lengthy debate with God, and God won each argument by demonstrating that it ended in infinite regress. Dick considering ending the *Exegesis* with this revelation but was nevertheless compelled to continue.

In 1979, the apartments in Dick's building had been changed to expensive condos, and as a result, most of the other residents were unable to remain in the building. These included Doris Sauter. Sauter's move out of Dick's apartment complex severed Dick from his closest source of support. In a December 27, 1980, letter, Dick writes that he spent Christmas Eve alone in self-imposed isolation, drinking Scotch and smoking marijuana. On Christmas Day, Dick awoke feeling devastated. Desperate for companionship, Dick called his daughter Laura repeatedly, but he could not reach her. He portrays her as the most important person in his life, although notes that he has seen her for only seven days in her sixteen-year life. Dick writes: "I have lost so many people that I loved that I no longer remember who I've lost."

Moments like these in Dick's late years underscore how inflexible his habit of isolation had become. If he had wished to spend the holidays with company, there was no shortage of family and friends who would have been happy to have him. Although Dick was still moody, his warmth and sense of humor were attractive to those who knew him. As his ex-wife Anne put it, "He had fantastic charisma . . . the jokes he cracked were so funny." Dick was not ostracized by his social world, but by his own choice. Donald Winnicott, a British therapist, writes of withdrawn people who are similarly torn between feeling impinged upon by other people when together with them, and desperately lonely when apart from them. Winnicott observed that these patients often seem to lack a stable sense of self. According to Winnicott, because of early trauma in the mother–child relationship, they suffer from fears of being impinged upon by the personalities of other people. To cope, they react by compliantly shapeshifting their personalities to match the expectations of whomever they interact with. This shapeshifting protects and hides the true self from other people. In extreme cases, such compliant responses can establish what Winnicott calls a "false self." Relationships with other people are managed by means of phony responses and the true self is hidden. Feelings of futility and unreality result. One of Dick's interviewers who met him in 1980, *Slash* magazine's Nicole Panter, later said that Dick "found it hard to believe that anyone could like him for himself." Winnicott notes that for highly intelligent people, the false self is often built up out of intellectual activity that is detached from the flow of lived experience. In creative people, the false self can use creative shapeshifting as a substitute for true-self spontaneity and aliveness. From Winnicott's perspective, then, one could view Dick's tendency to imaginatively prevaricate as a false-self substitute for true-self spontaneity. Because Dick felt his true self to be both fragile and unlovable, he presented friends and interviewers with a series of imaginary false selves, conjured up in response to the expectations of the other person.

A key idea in Winnicott's conception of the false self is that the person with a false self perceives other people conflictually. Because of the fragility of the self and its vulnerability to traumatic impingement by the personalities of others, other people are dangerous. Yet, because the true self is cut off from others, the need for emotional contact can grow desperately strong. As a result of this conflict, the withdrawn person can be trapped in a zigzag pattern of social withdrawal alternating with a craving for contact. That kind of conflictual pattern became increasingly evident in Dick's life in the late 1970s and 1980s. During that period, he frequently reached out to family and friends, only to cancel plans to spend time with them at the last moment. He wrote effusive letters to his children and ex-wives, blasting them with love and generosity, but rarely followed up with concrete steps that would bring them closer to him. Dick's rationalizations abound. He cites financial problems that make him unable to travel and health problems that keep him housebound, and gives various other excuses for avoiding his loved ones. Dick writes that he feels himself contracting, as if his body were conserving energy in anticipation of death. Indeed, Dick's legendary productivity slowed in his last years. Contrasting with the period in the late 1960s in which he wrote over a dozen novels a year, he now produced one novel a year at most.

Dick continued to take multiple psychiatric medications. In 1980 he was on a psychotropic cocktail comprising two different tricyclic antidepressants, Elavil and Sinequan, as well as an anti-anxiety medication, Tranxene. It seems that at some point in the late 1970s and early 1980s Dick was able to wean himself off the antipsychotic drug Stelazine, perhaps because he had reduced his amphetamine use. He no longer needed Stelazine to contain the paranoia that had exploded when he gulped down amphetamines by the handful. Elavil and Sinequan can be helpful in the short term, but long-term use can cause changes in the brain's neurotransmitter system that paradoxically increase the chronicity of depression. Tranxene, a sedative effective at reducing anxiety in the short term, is legally classified as a controlled substance because of its addictive properties. Like many psychiatric drugs, those Dick took were double-edged swords that provided temporary relief at the expense of long-term impairment. Aware of this problem, he made a dramatic attempt to reduce his dependence on psychiatric medications during the same year. According to his friend K. W. Jeter, Dick discontinued the drugs and was immediately hit by a rebound depression so fierce he could hardly speak. Nevertheless, Jeter reports, Dick outlasted the withdrawal through sheer willpower.

In 1981, Dick's book *Do Androids Dream of Electric Sheep?* was adapted into the Hollywood movie *Blade Runner*, the first of what were to be numerous big-screen adaptations of his stories. Although Dick was initially disdainful of the screenplay adaptation, the stardust of his involvement in a major motion picture swept him away. However, his actual participation was minimal. He met with the cast and director only once, when the studio invited him to a screening showing the special effects of the film.

Despite Dick's growing acclaim and financial success, his self-destructive acts continued. In the beginning of September 1981, he read in a newsletter of two other writers who had suddenly died from heart attacks. Reminded of his own heart condition, Dick saw the two deceased writers as reflections of himself. He was overwhelmed by fear of death and by resentment toward the murderous stress of the writer's lifestyle. In protest, Dick slammed his car into the support pole of a parking garage. In a September 4, 1981, letter to the editor of the newsletter, Dick writes, "I wanted to protest the two heart attacks . . . I wanted to protest my own enslavement to decades of writing in order to pay spousal support, child support, send my older daughter to Stanford, my youngest boy to a private school, buy my ex-wife Tessa a $150,000 house— meet deadlines . . . all the long distance phone calls." He further writes that the reward for the life of a writer is "not happiness but sudden death or disability." Dick mentions feeling immensely calm as he saw his car hitting the pole. He thought, with relief, that finally he would be able to rest. Dick survived the crash with a painful leg injury.

In subsequent letters in September, Dick complained of the pressures of his career. He wrote to Paul Williams that involvement in a major movie deal had been his "undoing." Although Dick continued to complain of pervasive feelings of exhaustion, he could not seem to stop his mind from speeding along. He continued to work on the *Exegesis* in fits and starts, aligning it with the theology of Martin Luther and the concept of the body of Christ. Luther's doctrine holds that the ascended body of Christ is ubiquitous, much like Zebra. The smallest stone, the tiniest speck of dirt, all participate in the mystical body of Christ.

On September 17, 1981, Dick had his famous Tagore vision. In the vision a savior appeared, portrayed as a Sri Lankan veterinarian named Tagore. Tagore's legs appeared burned and crippled, and he was unable to walk. The vision indicated that Tagore had taken on the sins of mankind, specifically ecological sins such as the dumping of nuclear waste into the environment. As a result, Tagore was dying, his body covered in radiation burns. If human beings continued to pollute the oceans, Tagore would perish. "The incredible sweetness about him," Dick writes in a September 19 letter to Paul Williams, "surpassed anything I have ever experienced. It was like music and perfume and colors—yet more." Dick announced his vision in a letter to a fan magazine and sent photocopies of the letter to eighty-four people, fans and friends alike. In the letter, he adds that since the ecosystem is inhabited by the body of Christ, destruction of the ecosystem also destroys Christ. From this perspective, environmental pollution is crucifixion on a grand scale. Later, Dick wondered why he mailed the letter.

In a September 20 interview with Gregg Rickman, Dick elaborates. Dick claims that after he sent the Tagore letter he received a phone call from a psychic who told him his vision meant he was physically ill and needed care. He was Tagore, and it was his body that was being destroyed. Dick concedes this to be partly true. He admits to Rickman that he had a painful burning sensation that made it difficult to walk. His interviewer recommends that he seek a medical evaluation. Dick replies that he received a partial evaluation that detected liver and cardiovascular problems, but that ultimately "I really don't want to know what is the matter with me."

In the *Exegesis*, Dick offers a more comprehensive reading of the Tagore vision. He notes that his twin sister Jane died after her legs were badly burned, just as Tagore's legs were in his vision. Dick therefore interprets his vision as a depiction of the key spiritual problem of the meaning of senseless suffering in the world. His sister's senseless death is, for him, the prototypical example of meaningless suffering. To spiritually cope with the suffering of the world while retaining his sanity, Dick says, he must believe that God takes the suffering onto himself and has a plan to deal with it justly. Otherwise, he would be forced to believe in an unjust and ultimately evil universe—the creation of a demiurge or mad God.

Although Dick's vision has clear spiritual implications, one could also read it as a psychological allegory of how Dick's impacted rage had poisoned him. From this angle, the barrels of waste dumped into the ocean could represent bottled-up moments of nuclear-level rage that Dick let drop into the ocean of his memory, without resolution. It is well known that unlike healthy anger, recurrent rage can have a corrosive impact on physical and mental health. Violent rage places a strain on the cardiovascular system, speeding the accretion of fatty plaques in arteries and resulting in damage to the arterial walls. Both the rage itself and the energy required to suppress it place serious strain on the body. People who struggle with rage are disproportionately prone to die of heart attacks and strokes. From this perspective, Dick's dream could be taken as an unconscious warning from Dick to himself: chill out or die.

The warning had little effect. Dick continued to pursue turbulent relationships. He had a passionate affair with a married woman, Sandra, that lasted several months and ended in a devastating separation. His letters to Sandra are tortuously conflicted. In them, Dick seems to approach and detach from Sandra simultaneously. He idealizes her as a spiritually powerful and dazzlingly brilliant woman whom he cannot match. He waxes poetic about his growing love for her, only to then gloomily predict that the relationship will soon end. Dick complains that Sandra gives him mixed messages about the status of the relationship, but he sends her letters with passages like this one, from October 27, 1981: "in no way have my feelings for you dimmed. They are strong and becoming stronger. Am I pulling out of the relationship, then . . .? Yes and no. Please listen . . . You must read this carefully . . . I want to continue the relationship. I will continue it . . . I do not propose that we end the relationship." Later in the same letter, Dick claims that it is Sandra who will end the relationship, leaving him heartbroken. Yet Dick confesses that "it has a measure of the self-fulfilling in it, this letter"—that is, by gratuitously attributing to Sandra the wish to end their relationship, he ironically hastens its termination. As Sandra's half of the correspondence is not available, it is unclear how much truth there was in Dick's reading of the situation. Yet, in Dick's letters, elements of transference are strikingly evident. Dick offers personal associations to several traumatic breakups of the past, including the break with Tessa that precipitated his infamous suicide attempt. Despite what Dick portrays as Sandra's uniquely alluring qualities, she seems to him to have been one more in the series of powerful and neglectful maternal figures in his life. Finally, Dick waffles his way out of the relationship, sending three ambivalent breakup letters. Later, in a December 26 letter to Sherie Rush, Dick claims that he had always planned to break up with Sandra, as he benevolently wished to return her to her husband's arms. It was all just part of the plan, he boasts.

Dick then goes on to explicitly complain, in a psychoanalytic vein, that he spent his romantic life seeking the loving maternal figure he never had as a child, only to find that each new edition of this figure seemed to transform into the cruel mother of his history. Dick was addicted to love, in its most thrilling and risky varieties. His letters to Sandra indicate that he perceived her as a spiritual portal granting him access to his innermost self: another Jungian anima figure. In a November 4 letter, he writes: "You were my doorway to reality, to the actual world; you took me out my own mind and introduced me to yourself and to what is actual." These remarks are reminiscent of the love letters to Anne in which he had placed her in the role of his savior. For Dick, Sandra was similarly not only a person, but a way out. His relationships, like his *Exegesis*, continued to be driven by soteriological themes. He was searching not only for sex or romantic love, but more basically for existential rescue. Sandra was the last figure in Dick's life who appeared to offer the tantalizing opportunity for spiritual transformation by way of ecstatic love. But as usual, the door opened and then shut for good. The actual relationship had lasted less than three weeks.

Dick's life remained intense, and the *Exegesis* kept piling up. In the last entries, Dick discovers that amidst all the second-guessing and self-doubt, he has found one consistent motif: salvation. 2-3-74 and its aftermath, Dick decides, was all part of a "program" in which VALIS plays the role of savior. Then, Dick notes that since he identifies VALIS with his deceased twin sister, Jane, VALIS's arrival relieves Dick of his lifelong guilt over Jane's death. Jane did not die after all but lives on eternally in VALIS. No death, no guilt. Dick also writes of a profound sense of integration of his spiritual and corporeal aspects. Spirit and body are one. Finally, he feels whole.

On February 17, Dick's biographer Gregg Rickman recorded a long series of conversations with him on philosophy and salvation. Dick is preoccupied with a cult figure, Benjamin Creme, who had recently proclaimed in a radio interview that he received telepathic messages indicating Christ had returned and would present himself to the world in June 1982. Dick links Creme's revelations to his own prophetic musings about the incipient return of a messianic figure, which he had variously identified as Tagore, Buddha, Apollo, or Christ. Dick proposes that he and Creme are tuned to the same telepathic wavelength, listening in on the same messianic signal. Amplifying the theme of integration that had emerged in his latest *Exegesis* entries, Dick tells Rickman that the new messiah represents a "great synthesis" of secular and religious aspects of life.

Creme's hopes for world salvation would prove to be disappointed. June 1982 was to come and go without any special messianic spectacle. Dick did not live to witness Creme's failure, however. The day after his last interview with Rickman, he was felled by a sudden stroke and found on the floor by neighbors. He was rushed to the hospital, but after a rapid series of additional strokes, he lapsed into a coma. After five days with no brain activity, Dick's body was disconnected from life support. His father took his remains to Colorado and buried them alongside his sister, under the shared gravestone that had been prepared for the twins when they were infants. The Dick twins were reunited.

10 | DIVINE MADNESS

In a comic strip entitled "The Religious Experience of Philip K. Dick," underground artist Robert Crumb sketches a cartoon version of 2-3-74. In Crumb's illustrations, Dick's head is surrounded by waves of energy radiating outward from his forehead, and Dick is encircled by streams of fire. In his narration of the story, Crumb asks, as Dick often did, "Was it the onset of acute schizophrenia, or was it a genuine mystical revelation, and then again, is there any difference?" Like other Philip K. Dick commentators, Crumb implies that these questions cannot be answered. I believe, to the contrary, Crumb's questions are answerable.

In answer to Crumb's question "Was it the onset of acute schizophrenia?" I would give a definite "no." Yes, 2-3-74 had paranoid elements that resemble symptoms of schizophrenia, like the Xerox Missive and Dick's fear that he was a destructive machine. However, as I showed in Chapters 5 and 6, Dick's paranoia was nothing new. It can't be said to be an "onset" of anything, because it had been developing for many years in the context of amphetamine dependence. In clinical terminology, Dick's paranoia was not *acute*, but *chronic*. By 1974, paranoia was business as usual for Dick. It was his baseline.

That said, some might conjecture that on top of his amphetamine psychosis, Dick also had a schizophrenic condition.

I would offer several rebuttals to that claim. For one thing, it simply isn't necessary to posit that he had schizophrenia. All the symptoms some Dick scholars cite as evidence of schizophrenia can be explained by the amphetamine psychosis we know, beyond a shadow of a doubt, Dick had. Moreover, Dick's professional productivity and his style of relating to others don't match the typical presentation of bona fide schizophrenia. Despite bouts of psychosis, Dick was able to write forty-four novels and 121 short stories during his lifetime. When examined through a clinical lens, Dick's life history doesn't appear schizophrenic. Rather, the clinical themes that stand out in his life are trauma and addiction. Perhaps what is most telling is that Dick was not psychologically impaired during 2-3-74. If anything, he made better decisions and took better care of himself than usual. By definition, an *improvement* in functioning can't be considered a sign of mental illness.

To Crumb's question, "Was [2-3-74] a genuine mystical revelation?" I would answer in the affirmative. Here, I have to give several qualifications. Do I mean that Dick was genuinely visited by shapeshifting aliens and three-eyed time travelers? No. Do I mean that California is actually a camouflaged version of ancient Rome? No. Like most mystical revelations, Dick's was symbolic, not literal. In 2-3-74, Dick symbolically experienced pairs of opposites that are universally relevant, such as growth and stagnation, life and death, freedom and confinement, insight and blindness, and truth and deception. We may not literally reside within a Black Iron Prison, but we all can get trapped in lives that are imprisoning. Whether or not we believe God is literally invading the world to rescue us, we all sometimes need liberation. We may not literally exist in a camouflaged ancient Rome, but our lives remain subjected to the camouflaged authoritarianism of deceptive political arrangements. In that sense, it is symbolically true that the Empire Never Ended.

Moreover, although Dick's revelations may come across as eccentric, his *Exegesis* succeeds in demonstrating they are consistent with major spiritual and philosophical traditions, such as Gnosticism and Platonism, as I noted in Chapter 8. As Dick shows, his revelations also gel with the respected theological views of Teilhard de Chardin. As I proposed in Chapter 4, Dick's traumatic history prepared him to enter trancelike dissociative states from which he was able to access higher aspects of consciousness, vividly transform his world through the imagination, and experience mystical oneness with other living beings. These psychospiritual abilities helped him achieve classical mystical insights about the deceptiveness of appearances, eternal forms, the interconnectedness of life, good and evil, and the creative process. What makes the revelations of 2-3-74 bizarre and idiosyncratic is that they were packaged in the vernacular most familiar to Dick: science fiction. Like his novels, his experiences of 2-3-74 addressed perennial spiritual concerns in a sci-fi style.

That said, it is hard to be sure of all the facts. Because of Dick's later fictionalizations of 2-3-74, it is difficult to firmly establish all of what he experienced during those months. Some might wonder if 2-3-74, like the counterfeit burglary I explored in Chapter 6, was a fabrication, a made-up story to bolster Dick's ego, and not a genuine experience at all. And to be sure, no one but Dick was privy to what was going on inside his head. Nevertheless, accounts from friends and loved ones close to Dick during 2-3-74 jibe with the major points in Dick's narrative about his experiences. Despite some discrepancies in the accounts, it is evident that Dick underwent what to him was a profound spiritual event. The fact that he later embellished the story of 2-3-74 does not gainsay the power of the original experience itself.

Crumb's third question is whether there is any difference between mystical revelation and madness. That's a tougher one. Theorists propose that some mental disorders can crystallize out of incomplete resolutions of spiritual emergency experiences. In Jungian theory, psychosis occurs when the ego is seduced by the irresistible pull of mystical archetypes from the depths of the collective unconscious. However, although psychosis and mystical experience both involve archetypes, I would argue that there is a profound difference: whereas genuine mystical revelations open the mind, mental illness narrows it. An aspect of any mental disorder is a kind of tunnel vision that Medard Boss, the existential therapist, called the "constriction of possibilities." People with depression perceive only depressing aspects of their lives, for example, and people with paranoia are vigilant to signs of threats and conspiracies to the exclusion of benign features of their world. Mental illness restricts consciousness, rather than opening it.

If there is one thing clear about 2-3-74, it is that it was a mind-opening experience. Dick felt his powers of discernment were amplified. Although his paranoia was still present, he also became attuned to benign aspects of his world. Dissociative processes taking the shape of "spirits" like James Pike and Thomas allowed him to more fully access his own wisdom. For a few months, he took better care of himself and made more prudent business decisions. These facts are well established. The decisions Dick made in early 1974 brought real financial results, and Dick increased his income. There is also Dick's revelation about his son's hernia. Although his intuition of his son's medical condition was not as miraculous as he claimed it to be—based, as it was, on suspicions that he and Tessa already held about their son's health—it was accurate and contributed to his son's treatment. As wild as Dick's inner world was during 2-3-74, his outward behavior was *more* effective than usual, not less. 2-3-74 temporarily healed Dick's estrangement from the world, provided him with better access to his own wisdom, improved his self-care, and enlivened his sense of identity, transiently treating several of the major problems in living he suffered from as a result of the traumatic life history I described in Chapters 2 and 3.

Still, as we saw in Chapter 9, Dick's mystical transformation did not last. As he put it, the "divine spirit left him," leaving him in the state of despair that contributed to his 1974 suicide attempt. Saniel Bonder, a contemporary mystic, writes of how euphoric spiritual expansions can snap back into extraordinarily painful contractions. Often, these contractions include powerful resurgences of emotional problems that the spiritual seeker must clear away before further development is possible. For Bonder, the process of psychospiritual growth is a zigzag between expansion and contraction. Consciousness is like a rubber band: the more you stretch it, the harder it snaps back. Bonder contends that learning from these contractions of consciousness is as vital as enjoying the expansions. Without a spiritual teacher to help him cope with the bumps and bruises of his spiritual contractions, Dick lacked the support to cope with the agony of the divine's apparent withdrawal from his life. The massive contraction he suffered after 2-3-74 recapitulated the abandonment traumas described in Chapter 3, but on a grander scale. After 2-3-74, it wasn't only his mother and father who had abandoned him, but the divine spirit. I am proposing that during the expansion phase of 2-3-74, Dick was *better* than usual, but after it ended, he temporarily got *worse* because he was retraumatized by the subsequent contraction. The door hit him on the way out, so to speak.

Despite eight subsequent years of study and exegetical activity, Dick was unable to recreate the kind of spiritual expansion he experienced on 2-3-74. He occasionally had milder mystical experiences, to be sure. The AI Voice cropped up during hypnagogic states between sleep and waking, and meaningful dreams and visions occurred. Yet these mystical moments were more like tantalizing echoes of 2-3-74 than full-fledged religious experiences of their own. The Tagore vision, perhaps, provided a capstone to the aftermath of 2-3-74, integrating loose ends of the spiritual and personal meanings of the experience. It portrayed Dick as a spiritual martyr who sacrificed his own well-being to protect others, retrospectively giving his life meaning. That vision did not break open Dick's mind in the way that 2-3-74 did, however. Although it was intensely meaningful, it was contained.

As I suggested before, Dick's *Exegesis* is largely the inscription of his mystical longing. In a context of traumatic stress, Dick had a spiritual opening that resulted in a powerful yet temporary transcendence of his problems in living. The paranoia driving his earlier stories and relationships began to give way to a mystical feeling that what lay behind appearances was not malign, but a divine conspiracy. The optimism of that stance is reflected in Dick's later novels, in which benevolent aliens or spiritual forces take center stage as salvific figures. Although the spiritual integration of 2-3-74 did not stabilize into a permanent state of wholeness, it did result in a radical change of attitude that shaped the rest of Dick's life. He was not solidly healed, but he was changed.

Today, like Zebra, Dick's ideas have invaded the cultural universe, often in disguised forms. Hollywood generates an endless stream of Dick-inspired movies, often credited to him and often not. Themes of simulated realities and android doubles are now firmly established in the popular imagination. More recent films inspired by Dick stories, like *The Adjustment Bureau* and *Radio Free Albemuth*, openly introduce spiritual ideas. If we take Dick at his word that his writings are forms of living mystical information, then the spiritual expansion of 2-3-74 has not stopped but continues to spread outward. Perhaps Dick's story ends not with death, or even with memory, but with viral, flourishing, autopoietic aliveness.

NOTES ON SOURCES

CHAPTER 1: 2-3-74

The biographical sources on Dick I relied on the most are Gregg Rickman's *To the High Castle: Philip K. Dick, A Life, 1928–1962* (Long Beach, CA: The Valentine Press, 1989) and Lawrence Sutin's *Divine Invasions: A Life of Philip K. Dick* (New York, NY: Carroll & Graf Publishers, 2005). Most chapters in this book draw upon both of these sources. The story of Dick's meeting with Ridley Scott can be found in Paul Sammon's essay "Of blade runners, PKD, and electric sheep" which was published as an afterword in the 2007 edition of the movie tie-in version of *Do Androids Dream of Electric Sheep?* (New York, NY: Ballantine Books, 2007).

CHAPTER 2: DIE MESSAGES

The most comprehensive version of Dick's origin story that I could locate is in Rickman's biography. Various details were fleshed out by Sutin's biography, by Dick's fifth wife Tessa Dick's book *Philip K. Dick: Remembering Firebright* (Crestline, CA: CreateSpace, 2009), and by Emmanuel Carrere's *I Am Alive and You Are Dead: A Journey Into the Mind of Philip K. Dick* (New York, NY: Metropolitan Books, 1993). Nicolas Abraham and Marie Torok's theory of the intrapsychic crypt is outlined in their book *The Shell and the Kernel* (Chicago, IL: The University of Chicago Press, 1994). Ludwig Binswanger's famous "The Case of Ellen West" can be found in R. May, E. Angel, and H. Ellenberger (Eds.), *Existence: A New Dimension in Psychiatry and Psychology* (New York, NY: Basic Books, 1958), pp. 237–364. The notion of an origin story is inspired by William Todd Schultz's theory of prototypical scenes, as elaborated in his paper "The Prototypical Scene: A Method for Generating Psychobiographical

Hypotheses," which can be found in Dan McAdams, R. Josselson, and A. Lieblich (Eds.), *Up Close and Personal: Teaching and Learning Narrative Research* (Washington, D.C.: American Psychological Association Press, 2002).

CHAPTER 3: RETREAT SYNDROME

Information from Rickman's and Sutin's biographies provides the backbone for this chapter. Ronald Laing's most important book is *The Divided Self: An Existential Study in Sanity and Madness* (London, UK: Tavistock, 1959).

CHAPTER 4: BEETLE SATORI

The Suzuki book that Dick read is *Zen and Japanese Culture* (New York, NY: Pantheon Books, 1959). Teilhard de Chardin's best-known book is *The Phenomenon of Man* (New York, NY: Harper Collins, 1955). His paper "Forma Christi" can be found in *Writings in Time of War* (New York, NY: Harper and Row, 1918), pp. 249–265. Rollo May's most relevant book is *Love and Will* (New York, NY: W.W. Norton, 1969). The Longden, Madill, and Waterman paper is "Dissociation, Trauma, and the Role of Lived Experience: Toward a New Conceptualization of Voice Hearing"; it appears on pp. 28–76 of volume 138 of the journal *Psychological Bulletin* (2012). Although Dick's *Exegesis* was unavailable for many years, an abridged version was recently published, edited by Jonathan Lethem and Pamela Jackson (Boston, MA: Houghton Mifflin Harcourt, 2011).

CHAPTER 5: DOUBLE

An important influence on this chapter is Neil Easterbrook's perceptive piece "Dianoia/Paranoia: Dick's Double 'Imposter'," which appears on pp. 7–19 of Samuel Umland's anthology *Philip K. Dick: Contemporary Critical Interpretations* (Westport, CT: Greenwood Press, 1995). Much of the biographical material comes from Dick's third wife Anne's book *Search for Philip K. Dick 1928–1982* (Point Reyes Station, CA: Point Reyes Cypress Press, 2009). Dick's essays on androids and the dark-haired girl can be found in *The Dark Haired Girl* (Willimantic, CT: Ziesing, 1989). For theories of the psychology of addiction, *Essential Papers on Addiction* (New York, NY: NYU Press, 1997) is an invaluable resource. Emmanuel Ghent's influential paper on masochism and spiritual surrender, "Masochism, Submission, Surrender: Masochism as a Perversion of Surrender," appears on pp. 108–136 of Volume 26 of the journal *Contemporary Psychoanalysis* (1990).

CHAPTER 6: COUNTERFEIT BURGLARY

Most of the material explored in this chapter comes from Paul Williams' extensive interview with Dick about the burglary, which appears in his book *Only Apparently Real: The World of Philip K. Dick* (Encinitas, CA: Entwhistle Books, 1986). Information about Dick's living situation at that time can be found in Anne Dick's biography, previously cited.

CHAPTER 7: THE PINK LIGHT

I relied strongly on two sources to flesh out the details of 2-3-74: Dick's own letters and *Exegesis* entries, and Tessa Dick's account of it in her books, as Tessa was with Dick throughout most of the experience. Accounts diverge regarding some aspects of the experience, and I note these. When narratives conflict, I tend to give more weight to Tessa's version of the story, as Dick himself is sometimes an unreliable historian. I try to be clear about which aspects of the story of 2-3-74 are known facts and which are guesses.

CHAPTER 8: THE *EXEGESIS*: LIVING INFORMATION

The source of the *Exegesis* material I use is the Lethem and Jackson abridged version, as Dick's estate has declined to make the entire *Exegesis* available. Relevant theological discussion can be found in Gabriel McKee's *Pink Beams of Light from the God in the Gutter: The Science-Fictional Religion of Philip K. Dick* (Lanham, MD: University Press of America, 2004). The Lethem and Jackson abridged *Exegesis* includes a brief but relevant afterword by Richard Doyle, "A Stairway to Eleusis: PKD, Perennial

Philosopher," categorizing Dick's exegetical activity as that of a perennial philosopher in the contemplative tradition.

CHAPTER 9: AFTERMATH: NULL METANOIA

A respected resource on spiritual emergency experiences is Stanislav and Christina Grof's book *Spiritual Emergency: When Personal Transformation Becomes a Crisis* (New York, NY: Putnam, 1989). Scott Apel's interviews with Dick are recorded in his book *Philip K. Dick: The Dream Connection* (San Jose, CA: The Permanent Press, 1987). Dick's speeches and philosophical essays can be found in L Sutin (Ed.), *The Shifting Realities of Philip K. Dick: Selected Literary and Philosophical Writings* (New York, NY: Random House, 1995), pp. 259–280. The Platt interview can be found online at http://dangerousminds.net/comments/philip_k_dick_interview_with_charles_platt_from_1979. Gregg Rickman's book *Philip K. Dick: The Last Testament* (Long Beach, CA: The Valentine Press, 1985) includes his last interviews with Dick.

CHAPTER 10: DIVINE MADNESS

Robert Crumb's cartoon version of 2-3-74 can be found online at http://www.philipkdickfans.com/resources/miscellaneous/the-religious-experience-of-philip-k-dick-by-r-crumb-from-weirdo-17/. A relevant and readable text on psychospiritual expansion and contraction is Saniel Bonder's *Waking Down* (San Francisco, CA: Mt. Tam Awakenings, Inc., 1998).

INDEX